MW01644230

The Bridge

We Are All One in Love

by

Kim A. Warbritton

www.OakleaPress.com

Dedication

This book is dedicated to my parents, Harvey and Darlene. Thank you for the lessons, guidance and love. Rest peacefully, Daddy.

Amanda, Anna, Logan and Audrey you are all the best part of what this life on earth has been. You are my legacy, you are treasures.

Love, Peace and Joy.

...when the game has gone on long enough,
all of us will wake up, stop pretending, and remember
that we are all one single Self—the God who is all that
there is and who lives forever and ever.

Alan Watts
Born 1915, Died 1973

Contents

Introduction

At different times in our lives, I believe we all look around and wonder if it would be possible for more love to be offered and shared in this world of ours. This is especially true if we happen to be an empath who feels deeply about what's taking place on our planet today. There seem to be so many places that need to be touched with compassion, and so many people that need to find peace in their lives. Many turn to alcohol, drugs or food to ease the pain and burden of life. Perhaps the opposite of doing that is the course taken by those who turn their faces upward and seek solace in religion. Unfortunately, some who start down the path of faith grow weary and discouraged. Many backslide and resume the destructive habits that entrapped them before they began a search for meaning and understanding. I believe this often happens because people are taught to be satisfied with what amounts to a surface level relationship with their higher power, and as a result, they do not acquire the deep and meaningful relationship that can lead to a secure and powerful bond.

Perhaps the majority also neglect to honor their Higher Self. It seems to me likely that they were never told or taught that they actually have a Higher Self. Rather than go deep inside themselves, they practice faith on a schedule: Church Sunday morning, then Wednesday night, Bible study Friday morning, and read their Bible or spiritual books on a certain day at a specific time. They do the busy human things but neglect to actually fuel their souls and lift them up with a true and solid connection.

Establishing a meaningful bond requires approaching the relationship as you would a marriage. You must pour yourself into it every single day and do so thoroughly from the heart with the intent to create a deep, intimate, and lasting connection. This is because an ego, surface-type of intimacy can only be felt on a mental and physical level. The way to deep, spiritual intimacy is to connect with who you really are—your soul, which is located deep within you, beyond the ego self—for your soul is the part of you that's connected with the Source of All-That-Is.

Much to my surprise, when I finally fully connected with my team of angels and with Source, I learned that most of us in physical form have been and are living a lie. Even so, not all of us must have the same beliefs. I was able to see that we are all meant to live in different ways and to believe different things because humans were created to be different and to follow different paths. But there is one thing we all are meant to share, and that one thing is love. We are meant to share compassion with each other and to offer encouragement to one another as we traverse this earthly plane.

The world's greatest spiritual teachers, from the beginning of time until today, have all shared the view that the deepest truth of our being isn't something that belongs to a single religion or spiritual tradition. It is something that can be found within the soul, the true you—the who and what a person is that's located deep within the heart of every single one of us.

It is said that closing your heart to other beliefs and religions will cause you to walk in the dark. Doing so also closes a person off from building friendships or relationships with others who follow different religions, and this causes us to miss out on opportunities to have a deep understanding of the world around us.

When you are able to get out of the shell of your small self, you will see that you are interrelated to everyone and to everything—that your every act is linked with the whole of humankind and the whole cosmos.

This poignant quote comes from Thich Nhat Hahn, a Vietnamese Buddhist Monk, a Nobel Peace Prize winner who is also known as, "The Father of Mindfulness." He wrote a book called, *Living Buddha, Living Christ.*

When he was in Florence, Italy, a Catholic Priest approached him because the priest was interested in learning more about Buddhism. In turn, Thich Nhat Hahn asked the priest to share with him his understanding of the "Holy Spirit."

The priest told him, "The Holy Spirit is the energy sent by God."

This statement touched the Buddhist Monk, and at that point, the teacher became the student and vice versa. It was the willingness of both spiritual leaders to be open that led them to a deep understanding of who they actually are. This also led them to realize that no matter a person's beliefs, lifestyle, ethnicity, political views or economic background, every individual is truly the very same at the core.

Another beautiful and truthful quote by Thich Nhat Hahn is, "Until there is peace between religions, there can be no peace in the world."

This is what I am here to share with you in an effort to build a bridge of love. All you have to do is change the word "religion" to one of the nouns I used previously to realize we need peace in all those areas, too:

"Until there is peace between RACES, there can be no peace in the world."

"Until there is peace between POLITICAL PARTIES, there can be no peace in the world."

My divinely guided message is about being "The Bridge" that we so desperately need. My hope is that I can help you understand that we are all one in love—that as we open our hearts and break down walls, we will build a bridge of understanding and compassion, so that we can begin the process of bringing together all of humanity. We each are individual units of a collective of souls, and we are here to experience life in human form—in a suit made of flesh and bones. We all have the purpose of being beacons of love in what seems, most of the time, to be a world that is selfish, full of hate and seemingly beyond repair. Nevertheless, as a collective we can raise the frequency of the Universe by raising our own individual frequencies, and by doing so truly be in one accord with each other and with Source energy.

You are probably wondering who I am and what makes me an expert on such a massive and highly intellectual subject. The "who" I will be telling you about is my human persona in this lifetime—in this incarnation. The real "Who" is the soul within that is watching and oversees the physical me. To be honest, I am just me. What makes me an expert? Nothing really, other than I am fully open to Source using me in any way possible to share the message of abundance in love. That's all Source wants from any of us—to be open to being used for divine purpose in ways that serve others without the expectation of receiving anything in return.

Since figuring out my divine purpose, I have remained centered and have continued to pursue it through trials and tribulation. You, too, can learn what is your soul's purpose. I guarantee you can if you will search for it with a pure heart and if your true desire is to serve your higher power, and live in truth, sing songs of gratitude to Source daily, and sincerely want to be of service to others.

I'm not here to change anyone, I am here to shift the timeline. I am here to help create a balance between shadow and light on the earth plane. Please understand, I am not here to push against the shadow. I'm not here to get rid of it, I am here to help bring shadow and light into balance, to activate and awaken others so that they come to the Light and thereby maintain the balance going forward.

I have a relationship with my Source that I previously did not know was possible. I now love people—that is the biggest shift within me. I'm not perfect, but I have finally realized that loving other people isn't about who I am, it is about loving the creation that Source has made—doing so in all ways. I have released the negative aspects of myself that kept me on the hamster wheel of life. I learned the proper way to heal, and to let go, and to transmute my suffering into love for myself and the collective.

I now love who I am—the *real* I am. The "I Am" that is in God—connected to Source—the Essence of All Things.

I grew up in Southern California and was what you would call, "California poor." We always had food on the table and a roof over our heads, but it was clear to me that most of the time my parents were scraping by with three kids to feed and clothe.

I was raised in an Assembly of God Church, which is pretty much pentecostal, and nowadays, would likely be considered Christian mysticism. I recall people speaking in tongues, and one particular Sunday, an 80 year old wheelchair-bound man stood up out of his chair and danced during the "altar call."

The altar call was always the most fun for me. I was raised to believe that there were no other truths in the world. For example, if you died as anything but a Christian, you would spend eternity in hell. If you died without asking for God's forgiveness, regardless of your faith, you would also go to hell.

As a child I was terrified I was going to die... and go to hell. So, all the time, I asked God to forgive me—even when I had done nothing wrong. I continued going to Church off and on all during my adult life. But about seven years ago, I began to question much, if not most of what I'd been taught. Some of the questions I had were, If Christians are the only souls allowed in heaven, why would God send all of those other loving, compassionate souls to hell? Why would he send gay people to hell? My daughter is gay, and she's a beautiful soul, so full of love, and she loves Jesus.

I never understood fearing the wrath of God. Why would I fear, "He who created me?" Source is just and fair and guides our path with love. Source gives us so very many chances to get it right. Source sends us an angelic team, spirit guides and ancestors to assist us on our path through life. Source loves us all so much that we have an abundance of resources above and below this earth. An infinite amount of love flows to us every moment of every day. I respect the Universal Laws and also the commandments, and I believe we should keep them close to our hearts—because to do so is pleasing to God.

St. Francis de Sales said, "We must fear God out of love, not love Him out of fear."

I believe the "fear" that is spoken of is the same type of respectful fear we have of our physical worldly fathers. The fear of disappointing the absolute most important Being in our lives and Who is with us every step on our soul's journey.

I had many, many other questions, so I began researching and reading and googling. My desire for knowledge was insatiable.

Shortly after I started searching, I began what I call my, "spiritual awakening." Such an awakening can be different for each of us. It's an individual process, and once you decide to begin, your spirit team will give you exactly what you need, when you need it, as you progress through the awakening process.

I went through a honeymoon period of feeling extremely good and connected to Source on my journey, and then I came to and encountered, "The Dark Night of the Soul." That was a painful time, but looking back, I realize that it was necessary, and in a way, beautiful. I then began healing past wounds and breaking generational curses.

It'a journey that's ongoing. Every day I am shown in what way I've grown and the aspects of my nature that still need work or to be released. In some religions or faiths it's called balancing the karmic scales. So you might say that an individual graduates from one level, gets a break, and then begins to work on the next. This occurs when you have internalized the "lesson" the Universe wants to teach you, and you let the Universe know, either verbally or energetically, that you're ready for more. Then the process starts all over again.

Without realizing it consciously, we request to be elevated before an awakening occurs. We do so by putting out new desires. For example, we may want something, such as a new job, or to find purpose, and so we are given a new lesson, or perhaps some sort of healing needs to take place. In this way the Universe "tests" an individual in order to see if that person is ready to take on the elevated responsibility. After a few times, they know what's going on when they go through it. The emotions generated seem more and more familiar and it becomes a more rapid process—because the person has been through the process before and allows him or herself to feel what's going on. They release the resistance and allow it to happen. I can't tell you how many times I have gone through the process, but I've earned a few badges along the way! It's not an easy process, but it is very rewarding. I even went through quite a few healings and graduated several levels while writing this book.

Before I began, I spent three years reading religious texts as well as books written by teachers of different faiths, and I was able to hone in on my Clairvoyance,

Clairaudience, Claircognizance and Clairsentience abilities. I knew I had a couple of these abilities when I was a child, but I suppressed them because I was taught that such things were evil. I recall feeling energy from people who would walk by me, and my hair would raise up on the back of my neck. Often, I could feel if someone was experiencing sadness or depression, and I could see light orbs of white, blue and green floating around. I didn't know what they were, but later learned they were spirits and angels. As my psychic abilities opened up, I realized I could communicate with my Guardian Angel, William. I also talked with my deceased loved ones and have even surprised a few people by delivering messages from their loved ones who were on the other side.

Then I started asking The Archangels for help, and believe me, when you call on them for help, they are always there for you. You see, they want more of us to call on them in order to receive divine healing and wisdom. The truth is that I am writing this book with their guidance, specifically Archangels Gabriel and Raziel, both of whom assist in writing as well as delivering messages.

When I am out on a walk, I always tell Archangel Ariel what a beautiful day it is and say how thankful I am for the wonder of nature. I also call on Archangel Metatron to help when I need healing and to be cleared of any low energies, and of course, Archangel Michael for protection from harm. You can access them at any time. Just call them by name, ask kindly, and always say please and thank you with gratitude in your heart.

One afternoon, I was feeling low and could not stop crying. Intuitively, I knew it was because my higher self was pulling up ancestral trauma that needed healing. The day before, I'd asked to carry the burden so my ancestors could be free and move forward in the spiritual realms and be cleared. This action would also release me, my family and future generations from such traumas. I had not experienced the depth of the low I was in for a very long time, and because I am awake spiritually, I was very sensitive to it. As I laid there, I began to weep, and so I called on Archangels Chamuel, Zadkiel, Metatron and Jophiel to bring my soul peace as I went through the process. I pleaded with them to pour their love and peace over me as I alchemized all of this pain and turned the lead into gold. Instantly, I fell asleep, and when I woke up about 20 minutes later, the low energies were gone, and I felt higher than I had ever felt before.

There have been so many other times I have called on them with a request by name, and each time, they have come to my aid. Another time, I was on my way to see my dad who was very close to passing, I kept hearing the name Azrael.... I literally said out loud, "Why on earth am I thinking about the cat's name on the Smurfs?" I giggled about it. I continued hearing it, but didn't think anything more of it—not until he passed. Then I knew it was Archangel Azrael, the one who assists in crossing over.

I am a witness to what they do for those souls and what they will do for us. They love us deeply and want us all to know they are there at any time to help and comfort us, to bring us peace, to light a fire under our butts and even to help us write a book. That's where I got the name for this book, "arch" being another word for bridge. I was talking to them one morning while I was out on a walk. I began throwing different names out and I heard, "arch."

I said, "Arch? Seriously?" Then I walked a little further, came to a bridge and heard, "arch" again.... That's when I realized they meant, "bridge." They named this book! For this I am so thankful, because I know my purpose is to spread the message of love, and that Source has placed me here to be a bridge. I was told to say, "An arch is a bridge that connects the hearts of people so that they become one consciousness."

I am a woman who is known for cooking good food. I have had several food businesses, the most recent was to prepare prep meals and baked cinnamon rolls for coffee shops. I have had many other jobs in my life, all of which have been to provide service in some way. Little did I know that it was Source that sent me on this journey to serve with compassion and love so that I could teach others to serve as well.

I learned that I am a Master Number 11 Life Path and in doing so have found numerology and The Gene Keys to be incredibly interesting and helpful. I also have encountered some of my soul tribe family along the way who revealed aspects of me and my tribe that I had never heard of, one being that I am a 12th House Angel. I follow astrology and keep track of planetary alignment and moon phases, and when I realized what the North and South Nodes meant for my life purpose, things really began to change for me.

God created the heavens, the earth, the other planets, the sun, the moon and the stars. The earth is mostly water and so are we, which is why people say, "Must be a full moon," because the moon affects water. We all know things can get straight up strange for each of us during those times, as well as when Mercury is in retrograde. I'm in awe of it all, and having learned a little pushes me to learn more.

The Emerald Tablets of Thoth the Atlantean is my favorite reading because I like to digest it in little bits, and through meditation figure out what it has to communicate. I look to Eckhart Tolle, Ram Dass, Dr. Wayne Dyer, Abraham Hicks, Marianne Williamson, James Redfield and Byron Katie as teachers who provide me with spiritual wisdom along the way of my journey. Additionally, I believe that *The Course in Miracles* is a Divinely inspired book that I would recommend everyone read and read again.

From the time I was a kid, I've had dreams and visions of being an author and of speaking on stage. But never knew why, nor did I ever actually think I would ever do it. I suffered from imposter syndrome, and didn't think I was good enough. I'm not college educated, and I did not believe I had the right to teach or to speak publically. I didn't believe in what I had to offer, didn't believe in who I was, and felt as though I would never be liked enough for anyone to want to read my words or to hear what I had to say. Growing up, my dad would hush me because I would talk too much or too loud. This left me feeling that everyone would feel that way as well. Only those in my life I would allow in, knew the real me. The loudmouth, crazy one was just as surprised at what came out of my mouth as anyone around me. I have always kept my circle small because of my lack of trust and the fear of not being accepted.

During my spiritual journey, however, I let that go, and now I speak my truth and feel as though Source is the wisdom behind what I now have to say.

I started writing this book many times and deleted it every time but this one. I was afraid about what my family and friends would think of my beliefs, but then Source clearly said to me, "I have given you this gift, will you use it, or will I need to bestow it on someone else."

So I said, "Screw it!" and here I am writing a book about my spiritual journey, the person I have become as a result, and how the knowledge that has been given to me has transformed my thinking about all those who walk upon this beautiful planet. I have also been called to share how, as a collective, we need to take the steps necessary to band together and build a bridge of love. That's what Source desires—for us to connect to one another.

As we move forward, I will share with you how I overcame my false belief that we are all too different to have anything in common, and that it's best to stay in my own lane. Never did I think I would be reading about the teachings of different religions, let alone writing about them. I even had the thought, "What if I get hurt in this process because someone gets upset with what I'm teaching."

That's when Source said to me, "Is this about you, or is it about bringing others to the Light of Love? Trust in the protection around you."

I must say that I heard that loud and clear, and so I let go of the fear, stepped out in absolute faith and the knowing that I am doing this for humanity and The Divine.

I am writing this with so much love. I want to show each and every person that they, too, can achieve peace of mind, that the power to change is within, and that others' lives, as well as the collective of the world and the earth—*all* is within you.

We are all co-creators with each other and with Source. Together we can bring about the new earth—a new earth of love, compassion and beauty. We live in an exciting time in that the shift that's been predicted has begun.

Together, we will cover a brief bit of theology, learn what all religions and faiths have in common, and how self-love teaches us to love beyond ourselves, control carnal desires and human nature, and break down walls.

We will also address the importance of living your truth and that you have been chosen—are a "Chosen One"—to be here during this time on Earth. Together, we will see how peace will open the gate that will allow you to surrender to the Divine and follow a dedicated and unwavering path forward—as well as how you can open your heart, mind and soul in order to see everyone as ONE collective searching for and desiring the same peace, love and joy in life.

A few chapters will be about my spiritual journey and what came to me to journal in times of meditation. Throughout, I will share quotes from teachers and gurus that come from every faith, as well as personal stories concerning what I have experienced along the way.

As mentioned above, a shift is occurring. More and more people are now searching for Truth and guidance. Source has prepared me to serve you, my sisters and brothers, and it is my intention to do so with respect, love, joy and peace. This is what my journey in this life is about—being of service, doing so with love, and working for Source here on Earth. You and I are roots in the soil of life and earthly representatives of the heavenly realm. We need to understand and appreciate that we are simply different branches of the same tree.

Love and Light!

Chapter One

Same Tree, Different Branches

Einstein wrote: "All religions, arts and sciences are branches of the same tree. All these aspirations are directed toward ennobling (lending greater dignity or nobility of character to) man's life, lifting it from the sphere of mere physical existence and leading the individual toward freedom (higher consciousness)."

Einstein used an image of a tree to show how ideas are related—that they all stem from the same source.

In Jewish tradition, The Tree of Life is the Sephiroth. Its ten Spheres of Manifestation serve as "reflective mirrors" of the divine entrance into the human world. The Sephiroth represents the way in which Yahweh—the Jewish term for God, and what I think of as Consciousness—conveys Itself in Creation. The ten interconnected spheres and 22 connecting paths within it form what looks like a tree. The Tree of Life in Jewish tradition is about the deep connection between life and wisdom, which can be understood through God's teachings, Scripture and the Torah.

Jesus said that He is the vine and we are the branches. So, not only do you eat from this vine, you are invited to recognize and realize that you are at one with it as well. This means that you can help produce its fruit, thereby conveying His light and love to others.

The book of Revelation in the Holy Bible says that the tree of life is a reminder that God's purpose will not be thwarted. The tree that was lost will be replanted; the creation that was lost will be restored. This indicates that we can look to the future with confidence.

In a spiritual sense, the tree of life signifies that there is life beyond the physical plane—that it, the tree, transcends earth and heaven. This clearly implies that each of us is a leaf on one of the many branches. Moreover, we all experience the seasons of life: spring, summer, fall and winter. As Deepak Chopra said, "Life is like a tree, and its root is consciousness (God). Therefore, once we tend the root, the tree as a whole will be healthy."

In Buddhism, the Tree of Life symbolizes enlightenment—enlightenment being synonymous with Nirvana, which is the state of total peace one achieves when an individual realizes and truly *knows* that All-Is-One. Appropriately, the Buddha attained enlightenment while meditating under the Bodhi tree.

Once we realize that we all come from, we all still have roots in, and thereby we all are connected to the one God of creation—what some think of as the consciousness we all share—it will logically follow that, indeed, we are all one; that there is only One Life of which every one is part. This being the case, to harm or degrade another is to harm or degrade oneself. If someone has different views, for example, it is important nonetheless to have respect for them and to realize that they deserve every bit of strength from those same strong branches. The intolerance of different opinions, views and lifestyles, is what often results in war and anarchy, which causes the roots and branches to whither and die.

I was in meditation one morning and what came to me clearly was that rejection of others is a rejection of what you find displeasing in yourself. We find accepting ourselves to be displeasing because a lot of what we think and do does not line up with the essence of our true nature, and it most definitely does not line up with what Source sees in each and every one of us. The same God that is in you is in me, just as the same God that is in the beggar is also in the king. When we look at another, and we do not like or feel intolerant of that individual and cannot put a finger on why, we are likely looking into a mirror. The reflection we see is something we don't like in ourselves. It's likely something about you that you consciously deny because whatever it is is too displeasing for you to stomach. Many of us do this when it comes to religion, race and political views. Ego-fueled wars break out because of disagreements with respect to religions, which leads me to reveal what the followers of a handful of religions and faiths believe.

Before moving forward, we are going to do a quick recap of the histories of the different faiths. These are the Big Five:

Judaism, Christianity, Islam, Hinduism and Buddhism

Here are a few more:

Confucianism, Taoism, Bahai and Spiritualism

And that is certainly not all. Did you know there are over 4,200 different religions in the world? But 75% of the total affiliate with the Big Five. In addition, there are more than 45,000 Christian denominations globally; in the United States alone there are more than 200.

As I begin this segment, I want to say that there's a great deal of dissension within the Christian faith. Leaders of each denomination typically have opinions about the doctrine being taught by others. It seems to me that if we are going to make peace, for most of us it will need to begin in our own backyards.

I have been guided from the angelic realm to communicate this: "The God of Love isn't passive about love. It's pure, it's free of judgment. It's a 'I hear you, I see you, I feel your energy, I will understand you the best I can and accept you,' kind of love."

God's love for us is such that it is actively opening opportunities for us, and each person is expected to give that kind of love freely to others. Love your fellow Christian brothers and sisters of different denominations and beliefs with the same energetic frequency God loves you.

As we all move forward to create unity in this world, the teachings of "As Above, So Below, As Within, So Without, as the Universe, so the Soul" written by Hermes means that what is done and exists in the heavenly realms, is done and exists on earth. The energies you feel on the inside are what you will bring about on the outside, and the world around you. If you are negative, the energy you put out will be negative and if positive, you will put out positive energy. Your energy, positive or negative, affects the collective frequency of the world. One positive person can radiate out energy others around them feel and this changes their vibration. Then, their higher vibration will have the same positive effect. It's a chain reaction.

Accept that others may have different views about Christian teachings and realize that for all denominations the core is the relationship one has with Jesus, not the relationship one has with his or her pastor or congregation of believers.

I am going to start with what I know as the oldest spiritual teachings. What is amazing, is that it was written around 36,000 BC on emerald tablets called *The Emerald Tablets of Thoth the Atlantean.* Thoth ruled Atlantis from approximately 50,000 BC to 36,000 BC and later reincarnated as Greek god Hermes. He is also credited with creating the art of writing, as well as with inventing the calendar and controlling space and time.

As I read the translated book, I could feel the energy from it within me. What I noticed immediately was that the tablets and verses were much like Scripture. They seem cryptic, but when you really meditate on them, you can see that Source has never changed—not from 36,000 BC to the present day. I would suggest not just listening to an audio book, but to purchase the book and read it as well. There is something about reading the book out loud that touches the soul. It is truly beautiful.

One of my favorite prayers in the book is Tablet 4 Verse 26:

Pray ye this prayer for attaining wisdom.
Pray for the coming of Light to ALL.
Mighty SPIRIT of LIGHT
That shines through the Cosmos

Draw my flame closer in harmony to thee.
Lift up my fire from out of the darkness,
magnet of fire that is One with the ALL.
Lift up my soul, thou mighty and potent
Child of the Light, turn not away.
Draw me in power to melt in thy furnace;
One with all things and all things in One,
Fire of the life-strain and one with the Brain.

If you meditate on the beauty of these words and allow your soul to accept them, the understanding of their meaning will elevate you.

I'd also like to point out that when "Light" is used in this book, it means "Truth." "Fire of the life-strain" actually refers to the energy centers, also known as "Chakras," and in this passage it is the Crown Chakra that is one with your thinking mind. We'll discuss this in an upcoming chapter.

Judaism began in the Middle East circa 2000 BCE
Christianity and Islam also began in the Middle East
Christianity circa 100 CE and Islam circa 622 CE
Hinduism is known to be the oldest religion that began in
Northern India circa 2000 BCE
Buddhism began also in Northern India circa 500 BCE
Confucianism began in Northern China circa 500 BCE
Taoism began in Northern China in 550 BCE
Bahai began in Persia in 1844 CE
Spirituality began in a small town in New York in the 1840's

I would also like to add the religion of the indigenous people of America to the list. It is not recognized as a world religion, but I believe it is worthy of being one. The Native American culture deserves to have a place.

Here is a beautiful quote from Lakota Medicine Man and Holy Man, Black Elk:

> *The first peace, which is the most important, is that which comes within the souls of men when they realize their relationship, their oneness with the Universe and all its powers, and when they realize that at the center of the universe dwells the Great Spirit and that center is really everywhere—it is within each of us.*

Indigenous religions are ancestral religions of people who are native to a particular land. Native American religion is Peyotism or Peyote, Japanese religion, Shinto, and even Taoism and Confucianism. Hinduism is noted to be the mother of all Indigenous Religions. The vast majority of tribal societies practice animism, meaning they believe all things possess a spirit or a soul. There are many religions that fall into the indigenous category.

Judaism is the base of the tree of both Christianity and Islam, which are what's referred to as the Abrahamic Religions in that they both originated with Abraham who is a character in the Old Testament of the Holy Bible.

Abraham was the first Hebrew patriarch. He is known for his teachings and for creating an awareness of God. According to Scripture, he was called by God to found a new nation, and he did so in a land that was known as Canaan.

Abraham was unquestionably obedient. He is known for following God's order to sacrifice his own son, Isaac, as a test of his faith. As you likely know, at the last minute,

God provided a ram to be sacrificed in his place so that Abraham did not have to sacrifice his son. For this reason, Abraham is also known as the "Father of Faith."

I won't be writing about Islam, as I am not comfortable with my knowledge of that faith, but will include quotes from leaders of Islam.

I have read the Bible numerous times and hold dear the teachings of Jesus. I think many get caught up in the history of His time and neglect to recognize the power of his teachings. He lived a life for us to emulate. It was one of pure love, with no judgment toward anyone, and he was always patient and kind. If everyone followed His example, the world would be a wonderful place.

If you are thinking something negative about a situation or another individual, ask yourself, "How would Jesus handle this?" The answer is always with thoughtfulness and love. In John 13:34 Jesus said, "A new commandment I give to you, that you love one another. Just as I have loved you, you also are to love one another." He didn't say to love those who are like you—He meant everyone. That he was willing to give his life so that we could live and be free to love one another indicates the incredible depth of love He has for each and every one of us.

I have read the Bhagavad Gita, which is Sanskrit meaning, "Song of God." It is a 700 verse Hindu scripture in the Mahabharata and a beautiful story of the teachings of Krishna (the avatar, aka incarnation, of the god Vishnu). In this text, Krishna is serving as a charioteer at the Battle of Kurukshetra that is being fought between the family and allies of Arjuna, a warrior prince, and prince Duryodhana and his allies. Truly one of the most beautiful books I have read, Krishna teaches that one can kill the body, but that the soul is immortal.

The four morals of the Gita are: 1) to be truthful, 2) cleanliness, 3) nonviolence and 4) simplicity. Albert Einstein apparently carried with him a copy of the Gita. He said, "When doubts haunt me, when disappointments stare me in the face, and I see one ray of hope on the horizon, I turn to the Bhagavad Gita and find a verse to comfort me; and I immediately begin to smile in the midst of overwhelming sorrow."

Now let's turn to *The Tao Te Ching,* which translates as, *The Classic book of Integrity,* and also, *The Way.* It is a fundamental text for both philosophical and religious Taoism. The principles it advocates are inaction, simplicity and living in harmony with nature. Due to the language barrier, Buddhist monks used the text to explain Buddhism to the Chinese. Unlike most religions, Taoists believe that a person's soul dies with the body. *The Tao Te Ching* was not written to be a religious text, but its teachings do line up with some Christian values and in a sense it has become a religious text for many.

Frankly, it wasn't the easiest book for me to understand, so I had to supplement it with other books that explain the teachings it contains. From what I can determine, the basis of the faith is to cultivate non-action by observing the nature of the world. There is no God per se in Taoism such as in the Abrahamic religions. Taoists believe in the Universe, Yin and Yang and in maintaining harmony in the natural order of things.

I love the teachings of Buddhism. The teachings are beautiful, peaceful and endorse mindfulness. The Buddha famously said, “Life is suffering,” and that is what his followers believe. Meditation, spiritual practices, physical labor, and good behavior are the ways to achieve enlightenment, or nirvana. Buddhists practice mindful eating, mindful walking, mindful sitting, mindfulness meditation and the Four-C’s of Creativity, Culture, Contemplation and Community. Buddhism is a deeply peaceful faith. In meditation Buddhists say mantras to themselves such as when they breathe in, “I calm my body,” and breathe out, “I know this is a beautiful moment.”

The Buddha, which means “the awakened one,” rejected the idea of a creator god, and so for Buddhists there was no first cause—for them, the universe has always been. They do believe, however, that there are supernatural figures who can help or hinder an individual on the way to enlightenment.

The Buddha himself was a spiritual master, not a god to be worshiped as so many people falsely believe. He was known for great wisdom and what have become famous teaching quotes. One of these quotes goes hand-in-hand with being a bridge: “Radiate boundless love towards the entire world.” And here’s another one I like: “Drop by drop, is the water pot filled.” I take that to mean that even slow and steady drops will fill the pot. A slow and steady flow of love can also fill someone’s cup, as well as your own.

Concerning Islam, I love the poet Rumi. He was raised by Persian parents as a Sunni Muslim. Rumi was very wise and his poetry is in my opinion gold. I will share with you some of his famous quotes.

Your task is not to seek for love, but merely to seek and find all the barriers within yourself that you have built against it.

Yesterday I was clever, so I wanted to change the world. Today I am wise, so I am changing myself.

What you seek is seeking you.

The wound is the place where the Light enters you.

And my personal, life changing favorite:

Stop acting so small. You ARE the universe in ecstatic motion.

Don't ever think that your words can't change someone's life, their mind or their actions. Rumi is the perfect example of what they can do. We are powerful, and we all need to realize just how powerful we are. We are created in the image of God. That means we have every power and every bit of wisdom at our disposal. When we choose to turn away from worldly things and to alignment with Source, those powers will open up.

Confucianism is an ancient Chinese religion that started out as a philosophy. It focuses on the importance of morality and personal ethics. The founder was Kong Fuz, but in the West he is known as Confucius. You know the saying, "Confucius says... "

Bahai is a monotheistic faith that holds that there is one God, and that we are all one life or race. Because followers of this faith believe in the oneness of humanity, they strive for freedom from prejudice, equality of the sexes, harmony between religion and science to name a few of their objectives. Their goal is to bind together individuals and communities as humanity advances toward becoming a collective. A quote by Baha'U'llah, "He Who is your Lord, the All-Merciful, cherishes in His heart the desire of beholding the entire human race as one soul and one body."

Spirituality or Spiritual Living is believing in what resonates with you coupled with the deep knowing you are at one with Source. I am in this camp, and Jesus has been my teacher and Savior all my life. Nevertheless, I enjoy learning and reading about the teachings of all religions and have incorporated many insights they have given me into my everyday walk with Source.

Some spiritualists are more in line with Buddhism, Tao or Hindu teachings. Others follow no particular teachings. They are guided by their internal compass and intuition. Spiritual individuals often tend to be free spirits and free thinkers, and a lot of times they are looked upon with an attitude of disapproval by those who follow traditional faiths, but that doesn't bother me. I love all the woo-woo fun planetary, sun and moon astrology stuff and the idea of being in tune and completely comfortable communicating with the other side. We spiritualists believe in energies and that our frequency is the major factor determining what we receive in life. Some enjoy reading tarot and have the ability to scry in water or crystal balls or to write intuitively. We know that meditation is what keeps a person happy and centered, and that living in the present moment is what life is and should be about. We choose to give up our past and not worry about what can go wrong in the future. When we think about the future, it is to manifest the life we desire.

Since I started on this path, I have become a different person. The choices I make now are not the choices I would have made before. I'm more sensitive to subtle energies, for example, and now tend to avoid low vibrational people and places. Even so, I now feel more compassion toward others and a greater sense of gratitude for what I have than I have ever felt before. I love others, but now I take better care of myself because I know my true value and that I am at One with all beings. Really, living a spiritual life is the complete knowing and "innerstanding" that you are always walking with Source. You are never walking alone; you're being directed to walk on the path that's right path for you.

If you want to shift your way of thinking about how Law of Attraction or Law of Assumption works, I would suggest reading *The Kybalion, The Three Initiates*. Originally published in 1908, it draws on Hermetic principles of seven basic laws to empower the mind and transform one's life. I find it to be very close in its teachings to the Emerald Tablets. This is not surprising since Thoth the Atlantean later incarnated as Hermes Trismegistus.

The seven principles are Mentalism, Correspondence, Vibration, Rhythm, Polarity, Cause and Effect and Gender. I would love to go into each principle, but I think it would be better for you to actually read the book and to meditate on what each one means to you and your life. That, I believe, will bring more clarity. The book is considered a Master-Key for those wishing to learn and to unlock the basic teachings of esoteric philosophy.

When I was a child and well into my adult life, I thought there was one tree and one branch and all of those other woo-woo, as well as ancient religions were wrong—that all those believers of other faiths would spend eternity in hell. The only exception, I was told, was that some Jews would escape that fate since they were the "chosen people." There are three branches of Judaism: Conservative, Orthodox and Reform, so I wasn't sure which group would escape Satan's wrath. Also, as in Christianity, other substrates exist—so who knew?

While doing my research, however, I heard from Source and the spiritual realm that religions other than the one in which I was raised were not wrong, after all. Nothing that is done or happens is outside of the will of God. The creation of Source is perfect. Divine perfection is divine perfection, whether you agree with it or not.

Back in the ancient days there were no books from other places in the world. There was no internet, there was no way to communicate from one continent to another. The teachings of each of the different regions of the world pretty much fall in line, and when all is said and done, have the same basic meanings. As I wrote earlier, The Emerald Tablets of Thoth, in the time of Atlantis 36,000 BC, to the teachings in India, China and the Middle East—all contain the same or similar ideas. Many of them share almost the same verbiage. Some theologians may disagree with me about this, but I believe Source opened my eyes to this view. I wasn't taught this in a school room by a professor of religion. My understanding is of the divine nature. It came to me in times of prayer, meditation, or while driving and reflecting on world events. It came to me while watching how people interact.

Since I am clairaudient, I can hear the voice of Source as well as those of angels and my spirit guides. I can see visions in my mind's eye. I get a sense of knowing in my heart space and my solar plexus. Often I am given something in this way that adds to my knowledge and wisdom. Whatever comes always seems to fit with the understanding that we are all the same, and yet we are all different. We are all one, and we are all divinely created. Whatever a particular religious doctrine may be, it was created by man with input from Source, and yet the details will inevitably be influenced by the culture and the epoch during which it came to be.

What we get when we become one with Source is a sense of knowing what we need to do with our lives. We all have different jobs to do for Source on this planet at this critical time. I may be called to be a vegetarian, you may not. I may be called to be a plumber, and you a preacher. Whatever we are called to do comes with different expectations, and yet somewhere deep down in our souls we know what we are being called to do. In the larger scheme of things, specific religious beliefs don't really matter. What matters is our level of frequency. The human race is on a journey to higher frequency. Our individual frequencies increase as we follow the calling Source has inspired us to take on. Imagine how much progress we could make if we all let go of the need to care about what someone else ought to think or believe, and instead put our efforts into spreading love and compassion and raising our levels of vibration and frequency. I believe that this is what Source intends for each of us because the end result will be a collective of like-minded souls who live in peace and harmony.

Each religion or faith was given a teacher. Each teacher shared the message God breathed into him. As a Spiritual follower of Christ, my belief is in Jesus and His teachings, and for me The Holy Spirit is the energy that guides and comforts me on my journey. But learning about and seeing the beauty of each religion and the teachers from which they came has opened me up even more to appreciating my faith. It has led to appreciating the people of other cultures and religions and opened my heart to receive the teachings and understandings that come from every part of the earth—all of it based on peace and love. Because you open your mind and heart to another teaching, does not mean you have to drop your current faith and follow another. Even if you decide that's what you want to do, it certainly will not make you wrong in the eyes of Source. I feel as though love from Source is what opened my eyes and created the desire within to understand what other cultures believe and to do so with an open heart and an open mind.

Many have the image of God as a big old white haired Santa Claus type guy with a long white beard, sitting on a gold throne with a scepter who is disappointed with all of us, shaking his head and raising his fist, ready to send us all to purgatory at best—if not to hellfire and damnation.

Forget that image. Perhaps you, like me, were taught that we're made in the image of God. Well, God is not a physical man, God is energy—energy, aka frequency, that is conscious. That frequency is LOVE. That is the image of God we need to feel and trust in—pure love that transcends anything we have ever felt on this earthly plane. You literally have to be in the same aligned frequency as Source to feel this immense love. I have felt it during meditation—during times I have been quietly reflecting on the power, peace and joy I feel coming from Source. It's a feeling of warmth in my chest.

When you are not in alignment, you feel the disconnect as well. I am not fond of feeling the disconnect, and so I do whatever I can to stay in high vibration.

As I began to research, listen to books and read, I began to "innerstand" that most faiths believe in a God of Creation. Even if they do not, they believe in a spirit realm and they honor their ancestors, or perhaps they honor nature—all of which come from and are part of Source.

We are a lot closer to being the same than we are to being different. We see each other as being different and may become xenophobic because each culture has its own language, a way to dress, and its own cuisine. Each has its own holidays, ways to communicate, its own culture and traditions. But just as people of different ethnicities, lifestyles and political views can live on the same city block and get along, so can those of different religions. As we have seen, the basic building block of just about every religion is love. Love is in fact the true religion and faith. It's just that simple. If we treat our neighbors as we would treat our family, or as we would have others treat us, great love would spread across the world and great changes would be realized.

Chapter Two

"The Golden Rule"

In his book, *There's a Spiritual Solution to Every Problem,* Dr. Wayne Dyer says about generosity and gratefulness, "I get back from the world precisely what I put out into the world. As you sew, so shall you reap. 'How can I serve,' instead of 'what's in it for me,' how about, 'how may I serve you?'"

I do believe this is the basis of "The Golden Rule." How can I set aside my selfishness and make you feel cared for? How can I serve you? Often, when we give freely of who we are, we get the biggest gift—the feeling of love from helping another. We've all been there, and we all know how great that feels. It also feels good to be the receiver. It's comforting to know we don't have to face the world alone—that is security. This is especially at this time. So many of us are going through life in a state of confusion because of the energetic shift that's taking place on our planet. We are accustomed to living in a stable, physical world, and the elevation in collective consciousness that's taking place can be disconcerting, which makes this an important time to help others on an emotional level. If you are a Lightworker, this is your time to pull yourself up by your bootstraps and get to work. Everyone present in this reality today is here to experience the shift and to evolve their souls, and so now is the time to live in your truth and get to work to fulfill your role. You, as a Lightworker, are here on earth to help ignite the fire in others with the objective of having them take on and live in their roles—in other words, for them to find their passion—so that we all live out our individual purposes. That's why it is so important to look past our differences and to give others a hand up—because that is something that will benefit us all.

The one thing every religion has is the Golden Rule. "Do unto others as you would have others do unto you." In Judaism it's the same concept, "Love your neighbor as yourself; I am the Lord." In Islam it is considered the ethics of reciprocity. Its followers are called upon to treat others the way they want to be treated. Hindu says, "Wish for others, what you wish for yourself." Buddhism says, "Whatever is disagreeable to yourself, do not do unto others." Taoism teaches that the loss or gain experienced by another, is also your loss or gain. In Native Spirituality the sayings are, "We are as much alive, as we keep the earth alive," and "Respect for all life is the foundation."

The "Declaration Toward a Global Ethic" from the Parliament of the World's Religions proclaimed "The Golden Rule" as the common principle. The initial Declaration was signed by 143 leaders of the world's major faiths. It is a principle in the philosophical field of ethics. It is a rule that aims to help people behave toward each other in a manner that is morally good.

There is a rule now called, "The Platinum Rule." It is to treat others not how you wish to be treated, but to treat them how THEY want to be treated. I believe this is a beautiful concept because it takes the "me" out of treating people with respect and dignity and puts it on treating someone how they as an individual would like to be treated. Not everyone wants to be treated the way you do, and so this makes you go a little deeper to learn how someone in your life would like to be treated.

There is also the "Titanium Rule" that's even better than the Platinum Rule. It is, "Treat people better than they expect to be treated." And finally, there's the Diamond Rule: "Treat others as they wish for YOU to treat them."

I say, just be kind, compassionate and humble enough to show respect even in the face of disagreements. In today's society, most people rarely look beyond ourselves in an attempt to form a basic understanding of a particular individual. This keeps them from forming healthy, communicative relationships. Imagine if God was too busy and didn't have time to care about what you bring to Him in prayer—that He instead he said to you, "I'm a little busy right now. Please leave a message. I'll get back to you as soon as I can." Then imagine that when He finally does have a moment, He's only half listening, only concerned about what He's going to get out of it. Often, that's how we treat those who are the closest to us.

I'll also leave you with this: Source is with us all of the time, but so often we simply turn on the answering machine and say, "Hey, Source, I'll get back to you when I'm not so busy." When that's the case, our treatment of others, including Source, is pretty muddied, and our ability to be that bridge is washed out.

In the folklore of several cultures "The Golden Rule" is depicted by the allegory of the long spoons. It's a parable that displays the difference between right and wrong (duality) by forcing people to eat with long spoons. It takes place in heaven and in hell. In both locations, each person was given a plate of food and a long spoon. Those in hell do not help each other, and they all starve to death. In heaven people feed each other across the table, and everyone is satisfied. The story is meant to teach us about having the heart to serve and work together for the common good—to do for others as you want them to do for you.

When I was a little girl about six or seven years old, my dad tried to teach me The Golden Rule. I remember looking him straight in the eye and saying, "I did! I treated him (my brother) the way he treated me!"

My dad really tried to get me to understand, but I was always a willful child who had a mind of my own. But that's what made sense to me. If he treated me like crap, why should I have been nice to him? To my mind, that was clearly how he wanted to be treated.

It took me a few years before I finally got it through my head, completely, and another few to actually start practicing it. In my defense, my brother was, well, a big brother, and I was usually the punching bag. He would take straight pins and put them in my Barbie's eyes. I would go to play with them and look down and see those silver swords sticking out. As I pulled them out, I'd cry because, after so many times, the holes in those eyes got bigger and bigger. After a while I could see inside her hollow head. But I would get my revenge. I'd snap the arms off of his Star Wars figures.

Looking back, it's clear we were both just plain old dumb kids. I'm thankful we learned as we got older to treat each other better. We put the sibling rivalry to pasture (most of the time) and created a bridge on which we could meet in the middle.

This is how we, as society, need to begin—start by building a Bridge on which we can meet in the middle; then be there for each other. It's the first step we can take to unite every single person.

Since we all understand The Golden Rule, what's holding us back? Perhaps it's that the ability to love others must begin with loving yourself. That means we must start by loving ourselves so completely that we would never treat anyone in a way we wouldn't want someone to treat us.

But, let's face it. We may give lip service to unconditionally loving others, but almost every one of us puts conditions of one kind or another on our love. Often it's because we don't unconditionally love the person we perceive ourselves to be. When that's the case, instead of starting with unconditional love, how about starting with unconditional respect for who we are—our bodies, our minds and most importantly, our souls? Start with respect for yourself, then, over time, look for and find love.

How do we begin? We may not perceive everything about ourselves to be perfect, but at the present moment—the only time that actually exists since the past is gone and the future's a concept—I'll bet you'll find that, right now—the eternal now—at the very least, you are okay.

When you learn to respect yourself, you will begin doing the things that create change in your life. Eventually, unconditional love will come along naturally—at least as unconditional as we human beings can manage because it's true that "unconditional love" is a hard standard to live up to. Perhaps "tolerant love" may be an easier standard to strive for, and then, once we achieve that, we can work our way up from that as a base.

It seems to me it will also help to water our self esteem with positive affirmations. After all, what is regularly watered will grow. If you tell yourself that you unconditionally love who you are, it will begin to become your reality. Ram Dass said, "A lot of our problem comes from our inability to accept our own beauty and to accept the grace that comes into our life."

Often, we have a hard time receiving anything. Individuals as a whole, for example, seem to have an aversion to accepting a compliment about their beauty—especially their external beauty. We seem immediately to feel the need to point out our flaws instead of just saying, "Thank you for your kind words." Maybe it's because we are taught that it's vain to accept a compliment—that if we accept it, we're full of ourselves. Having realized this, I have begun to receive compliments fully and completely. If someone sees something beautiful in me, I in return see something beautiful in them. Such a simple exchange can build someone up and create a bridge of giving and receiving that blooms into love that creates joy in that person's life.

We have all heard the saying, "You can't love someone else, until you love yourself." I believe that's 100% true. We all go through life at least somewhat dissatisfied with our looks, our weight, our career or job, our finances or our fictitious flaws. I say "fictitious" because they are. I was listening to Abraham Hicks one afternoon and heard a phrase that I adored so much, I had to write it down. It was, "Our flaws are a part of our magnificence." How fabulous is that simple statement? My mind tells me that what I see is not perfect, and the result is that I cannot love who I am. And, if I can't love who I am, I cannot truly love someone else. Then, we get into a relationship we believe will "fix" us, and it doesn't work. Why? When you expect someone else to fix you, or you put pressure on another person to make you complete or whole, it never works. You are the only person who can fix you.

Abraham Hicks also said, "Is what I am thinking at this very moment making me feel good?" If not, you're out of alignment with Source energy, and unfortunately, the energy you're sending out is going to attract more of what you don't want. This is a key aspect of the phenomenon of self love. If you don't accept yourself, if you feel down about your very being, the energy from that will create your negative circumstances. Abraham Hicks also said, "The story you tell is evidence of where you are, vibrationally." Change your internal story and the external story will change. Be gentle with yourself. There's a saying that an ear of corn doesn't just appear out of the ground. The soil needs to be prepared, the seed planted, it needs rain and sun and the plant has to reach full maturity before that one ear of corn is ready for harvest. It takes time to reach a point of loving who you are enough to say, "I love who I am." It took me 52 years to get there. We should be hopeful, even for ourselves, in a world that often feels and seems hopeless.

Before learning what I now know on this subject, I did expect "that guy" to make me feel whole and complete. I should have known that even Prince Charming would fall short. Relying on an outside force to make me feel important, loved and cared for was not the way, but I didn't seem to be able to find what was required within myself. I suppose that's how it is for most of us, and that's too bad. When we don't love who we are, we attract and choose partners that line up with the way we feel. That's because the basic law of metaphysics is "like attracts like." You attract what has the same vibrational energy that you're putting out. In other words, you attract into your life exactly what you believe you're worth. Up until my awakening, after which I walked away from a toxic relationship, that is exactly what I got.

If you are a father, read these words carefully. You are a model of the man your daughter will choose. It's important that you treat her mother with the deepest respect, whether you are married or divorced. You need to allow her to have a voice. It's important that your daughter can go to you as her dad and have long talks about random stuff, and that she can snuggle with you even when she's 16. It's important because if she doesn't get that from the most important man in her life, she will find it elsewhere. She'll find someone who gives her as much or as little respect as she gets from you. If it's little respect, the unhealthy relationship she will have as a result will leave her deeply heartbroken at some point in her life.

My advice is just be there and be open. Allow her to grow and make mistakes, but let her know she doesn't need anyone there to fill a void because she is enough on her own. I have learned that it is better to be alone and keep your own company than to attempt to make a square peg fit into a round hole. I am now perfectly happy waiting for what is meant for me and the man who will match my frequency. Matching frequency is more important than anything else. It doesn't matter if you're a week apart in age, or fifty years, it's about how you get along in terms of vibration that makes a good healthy relationship. I now know I am worth the wait and that when my vibrational match comes in, it will be spiritually, intellectually, physically and divinely aligned to who I am. I'm also happy with my own company, and that makes for a healthy relationship with yourself. I think everyone should live for a while single and alone before getting married or into a high level or intense relationship. I believe our standards increase, and we learn to put a higher value on our emotional well being and our bodies. I also now know I don't need to pursue anyone. If they are meant for me, I will be pursued.

Before I ended a six year relationship with a now ex boyfriend, I kept feeling Source nudging me to break it off. Now I know why. As I mentioned earlier, I was a willful child with a mind of my own, so not much had changed up until I decided to end it. I loved this man with every ounce of me, yet I was totally miserable. The relationship was one sided—I was putting a lot more into it than I was getting from it. Once I was deep into my transformation and healing, I knew I was outgrowing the relationship. He, on the other hand, was not growing, nor was he awakening. There was nothing wrong with that—he was, after all, happy with his life. But I had dreams—things I wanted to do. I knew if I remained with him, they were things I would never do, such as write this book. For about three months, Source kept showing me reasons to walk away, but I kept ignoring them, and I continued being miserable. My birthday came and that night there was a super moon. It was extra special to me because it was also a blue moon. I went over to his house, and on the way I asked Source to open my eyes to what I needed to see, open my ears to what I needed to hear, open my heart to what I needed to feel, and open my mind to what I needed to know.

I got to his house, and it was a great night. I even wrote in my journal what a beautiful night it was under that full moon. I made a wish on a shooting star that my life would be full of nights that felt just like that one.

A day later I went to my parents house because it was clear my dad was going to pass. When I got back home after he passed and waited a week before going back to my ex's house. I just didn't feel like seeing him.

The night I finally decided to go, I prayed the same prayer during the drive. Once there, everything was completely different. It was tense and uncomfortable, He was verbally combative—I felt as though I was under an energetic attack. We were in his garage and I asked him, "What am I to you?" After six years it seemed to me I shouldn't have had to ask that question, but we'd never talked about the future. Marriage was never discussed, and plans were hardly ever made.

His response was, "My girlfriend."

Then I asked him, "What do you see with me in the future?"

His response was all I needed to hear. He said, "I don't know."

The next morning I got up, fixed his breakfast, his prep meals for the week, sat down next to him and told him I felt we needed to end the relationship. If after six years you aren't sure if I am your future or not, I wasn't going to wait around another six.

Thankfully he agreed. He'd been feeling the disconnect, too, and truth be told, over that six years, it was the fifth time we'd broken up.

I thanked him for the time we'd shared and the abundance of lessons I learned about life. We have remained friends on social media platforms, and I have to say that the break was easy for me because I realized that some things aren't worth the tears. Moving forward was my reward. It was the beginning of a new life—I'd found the last piece of the puzzle that had been missing, and was now ready to move forward in my awakening.

Looking back, I did believe he was my Twin Flame, but I don't know that we will ever find our way back together. Only Source knows. I am now living life in pursuit of my dream, doing what I believe Source has called me to do, which is to help in any way I can to increase the vibration of the world. To take this step required ending that relationship, it was the biggest step I've ever taken in my quest for self-love.

Following The Golden Rule first and foremost means treating yourself how you want to be treated. I began my self-love journey to healing by correcting myself whenever I had a negative thought, or when a negative word came to mind or out of my mouth about who I am. I'd ask myself, "Would I say this to someone I care about?" And the answer almost every time was, "No."

As I took up this habit, I began to speak to myself in a loving, non-judgmental way. Over a short period of time, I began to see myself as the beautiful soul I AM and the force I AM created to be. I began to write affirmations saying WHO I am and in Whom I Am. Then I began to tell other people about the beautiful things I saw in them. The veil lifted, and jealousy was lifted from me and as well. I could see we are all the same. We are all insecure and almost never see or recognize our true value. The idea that we are not good enough creates a barrier between ourselves and others that keeps us imprisoned in our minds. I challenge you to do these things for yourself as well. and I'm willing to bet that in a matter of weeks your perception of yourself and others will shift. Even the slightest shift can have a huge impact on your world.

Allow me to add a word of caution, however. For the first few days this new way of treating yourself and the world will likely be fairly easy, but after a while it may begin to feel like a chore. You may be tempted to stop making the effort. Maybe something you perceive as negative will occur, and you'll be tempted to throw in the towel. One way to prevent that from happening, I have found, is not to have any expectations concerning outcomes, or any expectations concerning how others will react.

Expecting a certain result can be the killer of self esteem, and it can also kill a relationship. You may have experienced years of behaviors and wounds that you need to break and heal, so don't beat yourself up. If you want to maintain a positive attitude, it's best to allow things to unfold in their own time without judging outcomes. In other words, go with the flow—even in trying and difficult times. For me personally this journey so far has been five years of actually doing "the work," and the reality is that I'm still learning and changing. I now realize it's a lifelong process of choosing to be humble concerning my growth while seeking guidance by communing with Source each and every day.

I now know it's important not to judge ourselves if we fall short. There are going to be bumps in the road, and when we react negatively, we learn who we don't want to be and that the time has come to take another step forward. So think of it as an opportunity to make progress towards what you are striving to become as well as to come into closer alignment with your Higher Self.

I'd like to share a prayer I wrote in my journal. It's one I return to and say out loud on a regular basis. It's a prayer about surrendering aspects of myself that might keep me at a lower level of vibration and frequency. I want to release whatever prevents me from attaining unconditional love:

> *Divine Mother, Divine Father, Holy Spirit, Jesus, Angels, Guides, Ancestors and Benevolent Spirits, I surrender my negative thoughts, self limiting beliefs, anger, passive aggressiveness, hostility, self-loathing, being a doormat, not thinking or feeling I am enough, past hurts, future fears and fear of rejection. I surrender to you how I take things personally, my relationships, my life, my mind, my heart and my soul. I surrender my bank account, timing, my debt, my need for control, credit cards, car payment and house payment. I hand all of these things and my shortcomings in these areas to you to transmute them into self-love and to use in a way that allows me to serve You.*
>
> *And so it is.*

Truly praying, and then meditating afterward in order to receive an answer is how I have had so many breakthroughs in my spiritual life. It is a good place to start in order to transform yourself and begin to believe in your own worth.

As I finish this chapter, allow me to summarize a few key points, first by saying that The Golden Rule in all faiths is about loving yourself first, because if you truly love yourself, you will understand that doing to others as you want done to you increases the depth of love that you project in all your dealings and actions. It also teaches you to remove yourself from toxic relationships with lovers, friends and family. It increases the level of respect and love you have for yourself and helps you to understand that if someone is not reciprocal in their actions towards you, it is likely time for you to move on. It is also important to be thankful each day that you are a better, more healed version of yourself than you were yesterday.

Recognize also that your abundance isn't the car, the lover, the house, or the money you have in the bank. You feel and experience true abundance when you're in alignment with who you really are and are living your truth in alignment with Source. You need to treat yourself as you want to be treated and how you would treat another. As you do so you will begin to gain emotional intelligence that causes you to understand that what other people think—their opinions—are not important as far as you are concerned. They don't in any way change who you are.

As you progress, you will appreciate not only your own beauty, but the beauty in everything and everyone around you. You will begin to live your passion, find your inner child, and thereby begin to enjoy even the most simple things that life has to offer. In time you will learn to detach from outcomes, and that's when you will find your true power and achieve lasting happiness. You simply won't care what anyone thinks—you're just going through life being you—the true you. As you live this way, the walls of separation between you and Source as well as other people will break down.

I also want to add that Source does not ever separate from us. We separate from Source. The truth is that it's easy to pinch ourselves off, and when we do, a selfish, internal living condition can be created that causes anger, depression and self-loathing to bubble up.

Finally, as you live in the understanding and practice of "The Golden Rule," you will continue to make progress across the bridge that breaks down the walls of separation, and your egocentric self eventually will begin to simply fade away.

Chapter Three

Breaking Down Walls & the Ego

Sir Isaac Newton said, "We build too many walls and not enough bridges. Even paradise could become a prison if one had enough time to take notice of the walls." This quote can be interpreted as a calling to be more open minded and imaginative, to think positively, to look for ways to solve perceived problems, and to begin the process of making a negative situation better.

It seems to me that most of society is in a self-imposed mind prison and so asleep to the truth that they choose to stay in that prison. Even if the guard standing outside the bars offered to give them the key to eternal freedom, they wouldn't take it. They are stuck in "the devil they know, versus the devil they don't know" syndrome. In other words, their ego tells them it's better to live with the problems they have than to risk the uncertainty of change. Their minds are stuck in place due to fear, which is a hallmark of the ego.

So what's the way out? The present moment is the way. The present moment, which is the only time that actually exists, can become the portal to a new and improved future.

The spiritual teacher who has hit the nail on the head with respect to living in the present moment and letting go of ego is Eckhart Tolle. I highly recommend you read his book, *The Power of Now*, if you have not already done so. The first time I listened to it, I didn't fully understand it. Then I read and listened to it again several times, and each time I understood a particular passage differently, and I would embrace a new understanding.

Eckhart teaches that letting go of the ego frees you from the prison of your mind. Here is one of his most famous quotes about the ego, "The ego isn't wrong; it's just unconscious. When you observe the ego in yourself, you are beginning to go beyond it, Don't take the ego too seriously. When you detect egoic behavior in yourself, smile. At times you may even laugh. How could humanity have been taken in by this for so long? Above all, know that the ego isn't personal. It's who you are. If you consider the ego to be your personal problem, that's just more ego."

In his teachings, he also addresses how our human nature keeps us on the sidelines of life because we are too afraid to live. We believe that when we make mistakes or fail, everyone is against us or ready to laugh or judge us. That's why, he says, "Don't take yourself too seriously."

Find that small child within to find joy and laughter about everything that happens in your life. Even in the mundane, or what at times may seem catastrophic. It all usually works out in the end, unfolding exactly the way it should. Personally, I have laughed at things I would think, or at one time would have become upset about, because I now realize just how ridiculous I was being. For example, I would get upset that someone cut me off in traffic, and then would remember a mile or two earlier, I'd cut someone off. I never realized how unconscious I was until I became awakened.

One of the biggest lessons I learned was not to beat myself up for slipping. Doing so just makes the road a lot longer than it needs to be. Simply acknowledge that you made a mistake, that you had a thought or reaction that wasn't in alignment with who you truly are, or who you are striving to be. Be aware of that reaction, and then the next time you're in a similar situation, you can take the opportunity to react in a way that you'd like the new you to react.

After I realized this, I began to say, "Good job, Kim! You're doing better everyday!" Acknowledging my wins motivated me to continue to improve; it was much more productive than beating myself up over silly things.

Being judgmental is also something to be aware of and to jettison. For my generation, the one that was born in the early 70's and grew up in the 80's, judging people was normal. She's black, he's white, some weird religion, hippie, druggie, gang member, etc. Thankfully the world—even though it still has plenty of flaws—is becoming less judgmental of others based on what someone looks like and how they dress. Over the years, there has been plenty of social injustice, religious persecution, gay bashing and division between political groups and countries. It appears to be human nature to build walls around ourselves and to have egotistical beliefs. Labeling ourselves in some way, such as I'm a Democrat, I'm a Republican, I'm a Christian, I'm a Muslim, I'm right, You're wrong, I stand for this, I don't stand for that—all of that divides us and keeps us apart. It often causes us to act in ways that are not representative of our true nature.

Such labels are based on the ego. I honestly have an issue using the word "ego" because we ought to have respect for it. Your ego is the awareness that you are you. It's true, I believe, that we are all one at the core—all part of the One Life that is Source. But it's also important to understand where you stop and someone else starts. If you had no ego, you would think that you are All-That-Is and would not understand that others have rights, or that you would be better off to follow The Golden Rule.

People with arrested egos—those whose egos stopped developing at about the age of two years—are what's known as "Narcissists." They think they have every right to do whatever they want without regard to the effects of their actions on others—because in their minds they are all that matters, or in some weird way, all that actually exists. They go through life looking out solely for Number One without thinking a whit about anyone else.

Some scientists believe the reason humans developed egos was to keep us alive long enough to reproduce. That being the case, the ego's fundamental job is to worry, such as, "Uh-oh, where's my next meal coming from?" or "I wonder if a lion is hiding behind that bush." The problem is that an ego can be overly fearful. One that developed in an abusive household, for example, can hold us back from becoming all that we can be. That's why it's important to understand that the ego is not actually you. The ego is a construction that was built up from birth based on the family and culture in which you were raised. Therefore, you can change it and strengthen it. That, by the way, is the underlying message of Eckhart Tolle's *The Power of Now.*

Once we drop the labels and open our hearts to the reality that we all have different viewpoints, and that's okay, love will have the opportunity to flourish. It will also help to realize that we don't have to do what a timid ego is urging us to do, or not to do. The message it's sending us can be set aside while we consider what our intuition is telling us. The mind and thinking are amazing tools when they are put to work in service to the heart. The mind makes a great servant, but a poor master, especially when a timid ego has the upper hand.

One of my favorite Shakespeare quotes is, "There is nothing either good nor bad, but the thinking makes it so." We seem to believe as a human with an ego, someone has to be wrong or right. But if you think in the terms of, I have been wronged, I have wronged others. I have forgiven others, and I have forgiven myself—in this we can find freedom. Freedom is forgiveness and that opens us to our power, and that power is to receive.

Think about this. If you have a fender-bender in the supermarket parking lot, you're going to think that's bad, right? But when you take your car to the body shop to get it fixed, the owner of the body shop is going to think that's good—fixing that fender will generate the cashflow he needs to pay the rent and his employees. So, in reality, there was no wrong or right. It was just a matter of perspective and perception. That's why when something you consider to be bad happens, it's best to think of it as a lesson sent by the Universe to teach you something—such as to look in the rearview mirror before you back out of a parking place. Then forgive yourself and internalize the lesson you've learned.

When I was going through this phase of my awakening, I realized I held on to so much that I never forgave, even though I honestly thought I'd done so. How much I needed to forgive myself. How much I needed to forgive others. I now believe that you cannot move forward on your journey until you forgive. There's a saying, "Being bitter toward someone is like taking poison and expecting the other person to die." With forgiveness, however, comes healing. Healing is another aspect of awakening, but one cannot heal without forgiveness.

There's a quote from the Buddha I love, "Feelings are just visitors, let them come and go... Just don't cling to them." But most of us cling to them and end up in the fetal position ruminating about what he did to me, how she betrayed me, or how could I have done something so stupid? The list of what we overthink about and give too much attention to can be long. Our minds and egos not only create ridiculous stuff, they can cause health issues, anger issues, skin and digestive problems, and mental health problems. The list of troubles they can cause is practically infinite.

What many spiritual teachers try to get us to understand is that life will go along so much more smoothly if we calmly allow things to come and then pass. It's true. Left alone, most things are quickly forgotten, and then can we get back to business as usual.

How many times have you become stressed about something that never actually happened? Not only that, even when something you worried about did happen, time went by and somehow you were able to get through it, right? On top of that, often when we look back at problems we thought we had, we realize it all worked out for the best. This is especially true when it comes to jobs we applied for, or lost, making major purchases, and who we think we'd like as our partner in an intimate relationship. I know there have been plenty of times I have thanked the Lord above for not giving me what I thought I wanted. As a result, I've learned to go with the flow. It's best simply to set your sails based on the direction the wind is blowing and allow your journey to unfold. Once we learn how to follow our intuition and to do what's indicated, the act of begging God to bring you whatever you "need" will become a thing of the past.

My road to forgiveness started with calling people I needed to forgive as well as those I needed to ask for forgiveness. Some I meditated on, prayed for and went through a ceremony in which I wrote down what needed to be forgiven. Then I burned the paper and watched it go up in smoke. In my mind, that released it to the Universe.

Once I finished what I think of as my "forgiveness tour," I turned to my internal healing. When you are on a spiritual journey, it's not "one and done." Whatever you're holding onto has to surface. There are things within you that you're likely not aware of that need to be released. Often, they come up in bits and pieces. It may take a while, depending on how much you are holding onto, the amount of karma you have created, and your ability to stop resisting and to allow it to happen. I personally believe we often continue to suffer because we don't give ourselves permission to be healed. We get stuck in a state of misery and self pity. Perhaps we've been in pain for so long we've come to think it's normal and somehow comforting. It seems like part of us, and so we're afraid to let it go.

Here's my gift to you: A hall pass to heal.

Now you can say to yourself and anyone who needs to know, "I am healed."

If you start affirming to yourself that you are healed until you actually feel that way, it isn't, "Fake it until you make it." It's, "Say it and believe it, until you become it."

My biggest problem personally was that I carried a lot of resentment around inside me. I had anger, jealousy, and control issues. I had a "poor me" mentality and would never try to heal or forgive.

My dad was an alcoholic until I was 12 years old. He wasn't the, "Sit at home and get drunk alcoholic." He was the "Gone for three days" type. Thankfully, when I was 12 he had his "come to Jesus" moment and never had a drink again. But what he did have was his own childhood trauma, which he never overcame.

My dad pretty much raised himself. Both his parents were alcoholics, he was really poor, and he once watched a childhood friend get killed. His own dad was run over by a train when my father was in his early 20's.

Dad was jealous and controlling, especially of my Ma. I harbored a great deal of resentment towards him because of the way he treated her—I could see she was locked in a prison called "marriage."

Even so, Dad had a good side. At times he could be one of the most giving people on earth. I saw him give homeless people the shirt or jacket off of his back, and he also ministered to men in prison. He had a good heart, but he had a great deal of unhealed trauma, which is something I recognized later in life.

Ma never stood up for herself. I guess she found it easier to keep your mouth shut, her head down and go with it. I could say, "Ma is like Mother Theresa," and anyone who knew her would say, "Yes, she is."

She was God-loving, for sure. But her childhood trauma made her think she wasn't good enough and being married to someone who was jealous and controlling, she embodied the victim mentality along with a side bar of "poor-me."

I'm telling you the things I picked up on. Possibly they were generational curses, but whatever they were, I absorbed all of them. Here's something I want to acknowledge about my Ma. She is the one in our family who created a wealth of understanding about God, Jesus and The Holy Spirit. Because of her, generations to come will be taught about unconditional love, and for that I am eternally grateful. When it came to faith, my Ma followed her own path, and she stood her ground on that Truth. She never wavered and has remained faithful on her walk, and in her marriage.

Unfortunately, because she remained in an unhealthy marriage, it subconsciously taught me that doing so—sticking it out—is simply what you did. I believe that's why I chose to stay in an unhealthy marriage for many years, and why, after it was over, I stayed in an unhealthy relationship for six years.

I had a wandering husband which made for a tumultuous marriage that ended in divorce, and of course, what followed was the six year relationship I told you about in the previous chapter—a relationship that had no chance of becoming permanent. He had his own childhood trauma, along with pain from a divorce. Clearly, I was finding and attracting people whose trauma bonds matched up with my own. As I wrote earlier, "LIke attracts like." Thank goodness I finally came to the realization that I needed to heal, and that has been my quest ever since.

Forgiveness eventually came. First, I forgave my ex husband and myself for what went wrong in our marriage. We have since become friends, and for that I am thankful. I spent a couple years fighting the need to forgive myself for some things. But the whopper came when I had to forgive my dad. Let me tell you, I thought I'd done so, but I was fooling myself. By then, I was deep into my spiritual journey, and I thought I'd been healed, and was now in good shape and at peace. Then something happened. I got a call from my dad, who was suffering from congestive heart failure. He was being sent home to hospice. According to the doctors, he had anywhere from six weeks to six months to live.

His only wish was to see his family before he passed, and so I made the trip to see him. While I was there, the hospice nurse came to give him his initial interview. He wasn't answering the questions honestly. I later realized he was in denial, but on that day I became livid. He was leaving my mom with very little income, and I was afraid she was going to be left with a boatload of medical bills. Hospice pays for everything, but the hospital or insurance doesn't.

Well, I lost it. I yelled at him to quit lying, and I said a whole lot of other things. I left the next day, and when I got home, I journaled. I wrote five and a half pages about why I was mad at my dad—why I held so much resentment.

My dad never called me after that outburst, and I wasn't about to call him. I did call my Ma to check in. Dad called my brother and sister, but he never called me. Then he developed dementia, which came off and on—apparently, it's part of the dying process.

One day, about a month later, I was going through the journals I had written and came across those pages I'd written about my dad. I wept. I wrote him a letter of forgiveness, and asked him to forgive me. Then, with deep understanding, I forgave myself because I understood why I reacted the way I did. I'd been carrying pain around for years. That self forgiveness was just as important as forgiving my dad.

The next day, I was shopping at Aldi, and I got a call. I looked down and it said, "Daddy" on my phone. I answered, and he said, "Hey Kid!" as he always had done.

I wept in the aisle at Aldi as he was talking to me about the weather. At times he seemed okay and at times he would forget. I believe that letter had some power to it and the forgiveness broke down what had been a barrier and allowed Source to work. After that, he called me on most days, and during each call no matter what frame of mind he was in, I would say, "I love you dad," and he would say back, "I love you, kid."

His dementia continued to get worse, and he reached the point of thinking we were all conspiring against him. He had clearly become confused, and the goal of his phone calls now seemed to be to get info about what we were not telling him.

My sister would call and tell me she didn't believe he wasn't going to make it through the night. But miraculously, he would say, "Not today!"

When he got to the point of being in a somewhat comatose state, I could feel him communicating with me. His soul was hanging close to his body, but he was watching what was going on around him. During that time I could feel him with me, and I realized we can have a connection telepathically to someone who is dying. It's possible to communicate subconsciously with anyone, but as someone approaches the veil, the connection deepens.

About seven weeks later, I was on the road to see him again—about an eight hour drive. He was dying. My Ma, my sister and oldest daughter were with him during his final hours, although my sister had to leave to take care of something at home—she planned to be back as soon as she could.

I was about an hour and fifteen minutes away, when all of the sudden my heart felt as though it was going to jump out of my chest. I had a feeling in my stomach like it was being twisted. I looked at my Fitbit watch—my heart rate was 120, and I heard, "Look at the time." It was 3:38 pm. I immediately started singing Amazing Grace, a song I had not sung or even listened to for years. I got a call from my daughter at 3:43 pm that my dad had crossed over. About 30 minutes later I called my daughter and asked, "Did Papa pass at 3:38?" She paused, then said, "His last breath was at 3:37 and his heart stopped at 3:38. Time of death was 3:38."

There is no doubt in my mind it was my dad who twisted my gut and had me look at the time. He came by to tell me he was on his way to the other side, and that he loved me, that he had forgiven me, and to "watch out for deer."

Once I got to Ma's, I was able to kiss my dad's physical body goodbye, which gave me a sense of peace, even though he wasn't inside that flesh any longer. He was now in the spiritual realm and would come by once he was done with his heavenly check-in and processing. He now knew he could communicate with me.

A while after I arrived, we were all talking, and I learned that as he was taking his final breaths, my Ma told him to sing *Amazing Grace* in his mind. My daughter had been prompted to sing it from the moment she woke up, but had suppressed the urge all day—until my Ma whispered that to Dad. Through tears and with a cracking voice, she sang it during his passing. We were all connected at that moment, all singing that song, and yet we had no idea we were. That was such a healing moment for me. It changed my life, and I know it changed everyone else's life as well.

It was a long journey, perhaps made longer because I kept fighting it. I knew it needed to happen, but I thought you healed by fighting the feelings. I now realize that you heal by feeling the feelings. We are taught to push down our emotions—to sweep them under the rug—and I now know that is the absolute worst thing we can do. What this journey has taught me is NOT to push down my feelings, but to speak my peace in a loving way and move on. I am here to tell you, allow your feelings to come up so that they can be transmuted. Feel them—stop resisting and allow them to bubble up to the surface. Resistance will keep you from healing and achieving the ability to move on to achieve your soul's purpose and peace. Stop putting band-aids over your emotions. You need to air them out or they won't heal. Cry, get mad, scream, lie in bed for two days—then let them go. Free yourself.

I had 50 years of childhood trauma, marriage trauma and never fitting in trauma to deal along with other wounds—all that had to surface and be dealt with in order before I could be freed from it. And let me assure you, I would do it all again if it were necessary to bring me to the point of peace, love and joy that I feel today. The oneness I now feel with Source was worth the agony of releasing the baggage of bondage I'd been living with. Not only did I release my own, but I asked Source to allow me to heal the generational curses in my family so that my children and grandchildren, and generations to come, wouldn't have to deal with it. I then asked to heal the ancestral wounding. I went through five years of healing that I would not trade for any amount of money. I am free and so are the generations that will come after me.

As you begin the journey, promptings from your soul will come, and if you pay attention, you will know intuitively what to do. What happens when we finally lay everything down and follow the promptings is amazing. We are limitless. Our birthright is freedom. Our natural state of being is peace.

The problem often is that our minds can hold us hostage. We must make friends and be at peace with our minds, aka our egos. As has been said, it is possible to step back and watch the thoughts come and go. We don't have to react to them. A moment exists between stimulus and response when we can stop ourselves from doing so.

We simply need to retrain ourselves not to get caught up in negative thoughts. Let your ego know that today you're going to push aside negative thoughts and take Eckhart Tolle's advice to be present in the moment. That's how you can get in touch with your intuition so that it can communicate what you need to know.

Your intuition is an internal guidance system that can direct you to the path you need to follow to reach the abundance of love, peace and joy that is your birthright. You are here on Earth to find and experience love—the energy that breaks down the barriers and the walls that keep us from being truly free within ourselves.

Also don't let fear generated by the ego keep you from lending a hand to a stranger in need. Once you find love within yourself, let go of what no longer serves you. When you open yourself up to divine guidance, when you forgive what needs to be forgiven and heal those traumas and wounds, a transformation will take place inside you. You will begin to feel differently about the world around you, and you will see people through the eyes of love. You will also see nature and animals vividly, and the desire to reach out and help others will become second nature.

Saint Teresa of Calcutta, also known as Mother Teresa, is a Saint we can learn from. We can follow her example and reach out to help a stranger. Her life was one of never seeing the differences in people—of lending a hand up out of divine love and compassion. She was a leader who set an example by crossing barriers most would never have thought possible. As of 2012, she had formed a congregation of 4,500 nuns spread across 133 countries. That congregation of nuns runs soup kitchens, clinics, orphanages and a long list of other charities and programs. They give to those who are in need and would be considered unclean by the average person. That sort of love and compassion for others is what God has placed within the core of each of us—to be one with our fellow humans. That's who we are at the soul level.

Mother Teresa was also a keeper of peace. She said that peace and war begin at home, and if we truly want peace in the world, we must begin by loving one another, starting with our own families. She was asked once why she never participated in anti-war demonstrations . Her response was, "I will never attend an anti-war rally. If you have a peace rally, invite me."

She knew a rally for peace would generate a more powerful energy to put out into the world. On November 9, 1989, for example, we witnessed the fall of the Berlin Wall also known as The Iron Curtain, during the "Peaceful Revolution." This wall had divided Soviet Controlled Communist East Berlin and West Berlin. It was a pivotal time in history. That it came down proves that walls, even the ones we build around ourselves can come down due to the power of peace. I bring this up to show that the statement made by Mother Teresa is true, and that the power to create peace is within each of us.

The forgiveness and healing we allow ourselves can open so many doors. To advance along the path, we need to practice non-attachment from views that separate us in order to create peace between cultures, social groups and religions. Being open to listening and learning about different ideologies when spoken and shared in peace, will open you up to appreciate the beauty of our differences. When we find peace within, we can then find peace when sharing an open conversation with others. Our inner being desires this above everything else.

We can be fed by many religious teachings, especially when we allow Source to speak to us through the words we read or hear. In times of quiet solitude and meditation, we can come to know that love is the antidote to so many problems. We must open ourselves to receiving from Source the ways and means to bring about positive change and the power to break down walls. By doing so, we can be conduits through which The Divine can work. All we have to do is put our thoughts aside—shoo them away—so that we open ourselves up to receive the promptings—that's how we can create great social change.

Here's what I think is good advice. Turn off the news—be careful what you allow into your mind through television shows, social media and negative discussions with others. Excuse yourself from a conversation when the person is speaking ill of another. Talking behind someone's back is one of the worst cancers in the human world, and remember, if someone is speaking negatively to you of someone else, rest assured you're not safe from that person doing the same about you. I was the victim and the perpetrator of this sort of thing many times before I woke up, and when that's the case, you live in fear that what you said was going to come into the light.

Live and enjoy life with a clear conscience. The best way to do so is to be wise enough to know when to speak and when to keep your mouth shut. Living in fear because of a dishonest or fiery tongue is no fun at all, and I guarantee that lost sleep and fractured relationships will follow as a result if you allow it to happen.

I'll end this chapter with this. Allow the walls you've built around you to crumble. Drop any and all resistance that may be slowing the flow of what is meant to come to you in this life. Once you do, everything will unfold in a smooth, steady way, and you will feel the freedom to be who you are.

Finally, show others the same respect you would like to come to you. By doing so, you look fear in the eye with undeniable courage and thereby create concrete change for the good of all humankind.

Chapter Four

God is Love, Fear is Not

I am not here to change anyone. My goal is to shift the timeline—to balance the shadow and the Light. The physical realm in which we live is a duality reality and that means both Light and shadow must exist. We cannot know up without down, nor joy without sorrow, or white without black. Therefore, I am not here to push against the shadow, nor is it my goal to get rid of it. I am here to keep the balance and to activate and awaken others to come to the Light and thereby maintain the balance.

In order to live my calling, I cannot have fear in my heart. The lack of patience, the lack of love, gratitude, peace, joy and kindness all cause fear. That's why we all need to come together to share good fruits with others who may be seeking, others who may be lost or need a helping hand in order to find the way to step onto their paths toward healing and awakening. In doing so, they too can cross the bridge to unite all people in all walks of life.

The Law of Divine Compensation written by Marianne Williamson has the perfect statement written for this chapter:

> *Change our nature from thinking out of fear*
> *and limitation to faith and love.*

Most of the time, fear is what's behind why we choose to be against another religion or culture, or why we choose not to have a genuine understanding of other people. We love to stay in our little bubble of what we know and feel comfortable about because what's in the outside world is scary. Our little worlds are like a big comfy chair with a cozy blanket. Who wouldn't want to sit in front of a warm fireplace with a cup of cocoa and a good book? Who would want to leave that and peek out from behind the curtain to see what lies beyond in what may seem a dark and dingy world? But that is exactly what we need to do—drop the self imposed limitations and find the faith necessary, not only in Source, but in ourselves to create a desirable new world.

Instead, we typically create the restrictions for ourselves, and that means we need to get out of our own way and allow it to happen. Are we going to choose love or are we going to choose fear? If you choose fear, you are taking the wrong path—the path of least resistance. It is truly the path that creates barriers that keep you from what has been set aside for you. Fear is why most people won't accept anything other than what they think they know. I don't recall who said it but I agree, "The quality of your life is in direct proportion to the amount of uncertainty you can comfortably live with."

When I lived in fear, I pushed away what was meant for me. I was afraid the past would repeat itself. I was afraid I would be ridiculed, made fun of, talked about, cheated on, left again, or that I would fail. There were so many times I could have been successful at a business venture, but I'd stop myself before I started. I was afraid to be successful. That may sound crazy, but being successful comes with its own challenges.

When you live in fear, you tend to also live in anger and hopelessness. You ruminate on what will go wrong and procrastinate because doing something you know you need to do, or what Source is encouraging you to do, might lead to yet another failure. This causes us to push people away—because if you keep everyone at an arm's length you cannot be hurt by them. Yet pushing others away is exactly what causes the hurt.

We are meant to be with others, but if we aren't in alignment, as was stated in an earlier chapter, we will attract exactly what we are putting out. The low vibration of fear is why we attract people into our lives that we ought not to want in our reality—people who bring negativity and drama and bring us down off of what Abraham Hicks calls our "high flying disc."

When your vibrational frequency is high and in line with Source, people will be plucked, pruned and removed from your life to make room to attract in high vibrational people—those in your "soul tribe." Those with whom you can walk and talk with confidence, knowing that your daily interactions will be healthy. Doing so builds us up and keeps us lifted so that when we do come into contact with lower vibrational people, we don't lose our balance, and can instead show our light.

Nevertheless, be cautious of low vibrational people's energy. Unconsciously, they pull you down to their level of perspective in whatever situation may be at hand. Protect the level of energy you have achieved. Think of your vibrational frequency, as vibrational currency. You have worked hard to earn that currency, sometimes years, and to give it out to someone who doesn't deserve to have access to it or to you, would be worse than taking a million dollars and throwing it into a bonfire. Your vibration is what keeps you in alignment with Source energy, and if you allow someone to take it, you pinch yourself off and will have to work even harder to earn that level of currency back. Protect it like you're a Brinks security truck driver and your life depends on protecting what's in that truck.

If I listened to the few people who knew I was writing a book, I would have never started it. I got the "look" like I was on psychedelics, or the "Oh, that's cute" look, as well as the "Please don't embarrass yourself" look. If this book sells zero copies, ten copies or ten million copies, the fact will be that I got beyond what people thought of me and just did it, and that's what matters. I felt as though Source was guiding me to write this book, and doing so has also helped me heal. It's something I have always wanted to do, and I finally realized, I am an intelligent woman, and not only that, I have Source and a team of angels guiding me. Together, we are putting these words together to serve the collective.

We all have a story, and I would encourage you to share yours. Get a pen or boot up your computer and start writing. You never know if your story may touch someone and help them through their trials, or give courage when it's most needed. Doing so will lift your vibration, and you will have a renewed sense of what you can do. Trust me, writing this has changed me, and I believe it can help you and elevate your life. Simply start by sharing your journey and allow it to be used in Divine timing by Source.

Living a spiritual life means walking and in hand with Source, instead of walking the road of life all alone. When you do so, what and who is meant to be in your life will come. For a while when I was closeted in spiritual solitude, I thought I'd lost all of my friends and relationships. In reality, they were beautifully picked away from me during the time that I learned who I am. I became my best friend. I deepened my relationship with Source—as well as my relationship with my cat. I would pray and meditate daily for Source to fill me with love, wisdom, and the desire to do the "Lightwork" of helping the collective to awaken.

For me, being in solitude lifted my frequency so high that it radiated out of my apartment and into the cosmos where the Universe could use it to shower love wherever it needed to be. Once my mind caught up with my spirit, I was able to keep my thoughts in balance. If you don't allow thoughts that are opposed to what you want to stick in your mind, momentum will be created that attracts what you desire, including relationships that are healthy emotionally, spiritually and physically. This happens when you truly decide what you want, make a decision, write it down, and have the audacity to believe it is already yours. This elevates your body's vibration. Whatever you do, do not allow opposing thoughts to come. It may take a day to manifest, or it might take two years. Just put it out there and know you have it. As Jesus said, "Whatever you ask for in prayer, believe that you have received it, and it will be yours." (See Mark 11:24) As long as you continue vibrating at a high level, it will come to you. It's that simple—we create the world we experience with our minds.

Most people have an "I hope this works but who knows if it will" attitude. What they experience in return is mediocre at best because that's what such a mindset produces. I once told my daughter one day after getting a desk for my office, "I need to manifest a desk chair." We both laughed. But two hours later, she came walking in with a desk chair that she'd gotten from a neighbor who was in the process of moving and was about to take it to the dumpster.

She said, "I don't know how you did that, but here's your chair!"

It's simple, I told the universe what I needed and believed it was going to come in one way or another—and it did.

Don't fear, believe!

Confusion is something else that comes with fear. When we fight going down the path we know we ought to take, it causes confusion. In church I often heard, "The devil is the source of all confusion." Well, I'd say being out of alignment with God is a hell in and of itself and confusion is the byproduct. I don't give "the devil" any credit at all that's going on in my life. I'm full of the power of The Most High and can't be touched. I believe we need to stop blaming the dark forces and give glory to the Light. Words have power, even those we hear in church, and so rather than say something negative, why not give positive credit to the trials we face as being lessons sent to teach us in order to help us make progress toward becoming the best that we can be? I now welcome those tests and know that they will bring me to the point of graduating to the next level on my spiritual walk.

Don't be confused when a test comes along. Look to Source and ask, "What am I supposed to learn from this?

Please open me up to receiving the teaching so that I can move on to the next lesson."

Life on Earth is a kind of school. We're here to learn by facing and overcoming obstacles and thereby to move to the next phase and up to the next level. Remaining in one place and not growing is what causes the confusion. Our souls know why we're here—that it's to grow and evolve. It's fear that holds us back, and so when we allow fear to stop us, we lose what life has to offer. The lack of action due to fear or laziness, causes us to miss out on our blessings.

While writing this book, the food business I'd had for six years began to fail. Out of the blue, I went from making 130 meals a day to making less than 50 in a week. So I looked to Source and received the guidance I expected. I was guided where to look and what to do, step-by-step. The guidance was a gift, but I was nevertheless responsible for actually taking the steps and doing the work that had to be done. As a result, I was able to obtain a position with a company to which I would otherwise never have thought to apply. What's important to know is that before taking my journey, I wouldn't have thought to do what I did. But with the confidence I'd acquired, I was at peace during the storm—literally not worried at all. I knew I would be guided, and I trusted completely. It has all worked out, and now I finally know what it feels like to have unwavering faith.

When I arrived at the training restaurant for my new employment as a front of house manager, I was greeted by the general manager. It's important to realize that when you carry the Light within you, those who are "lost" cannot stand you because of your energy. I have become accustomed to dealing with this. I am a strong, independent and intelligent woman who knows her value because I work for Source. After three days I had to contact the operations manager of the company and ask to be moved to a different store for training. Instead of giving up, I adjusted the sails and asked for the help I needed to be successful in my new role. The operations manager was understanding, accommodating and was impressed that I stood up for myself.

My point is that the old me would have quit without hesitation and moved on. I refuse to do anything like that in my life now. I was placed there for a purpose greater than myself. I may be there to run the company one day, or it may be a stepping stone. But Source handed me the challenge, and so I showed Source how much I have changed, and I'm certain I passed the test. In the past, I would likely have seen myself as the problem, but now I saw things for what they actually were and did not judge myself.

Judging others is something that usually happens because we fear the unknown or we experience fear due to ignorance. In the past, I was guilty of judging people because of their skin color, the way they dress, or their religion. I am not proud of that, and I am thankful that I have been freed from the small amount of prejudice I used to carry around. What we all witnessed in the year 2020, during the pandemic, such as the social injustices against people of color, shifted my thinking, and my heart began to change. I realized to the deepest part of who I am that all everyone wants is to be free and to live the way they choose, to love who they want to love, and to worship in whatever way that causes them to feel close to their creator. They want to be able to walk down the street without fear of being pulled aside because of the color of their skin.

When we look at each other, we need to look through our God goggles and see how beautiful someone is and appreciate their race, or their religious dress. Beyond that, it is the soul within that's seen by Source. It is the internal part of us that is the true essence of who we are. Judging others places a mirror in front of our own lives and that mirroring is what causes insecurities within. Those insecurities are not from Source, they are the manifestation of an internal struggle—the fear of not being accepted, or even about being judged.

It's easy to be the judge, but it is difficult to be the one on trial because you are automatically perceived as being guilty. However, letting go of those judgments, insecurities and fears will open you up to a new, higher level of you.

One day my youngest daughter and I were talking and she said, "Mama, it would be so much easier if I were straight. The way strangers treat me and other gay people is terrible. What people say, telling us we're going to hell, and how they stare, is so hurtful. I didn't ask to be born this way, and if I could be straight, it would be so much easier."

So many people sit on their seat of judgment and never take into account how powerful and painful their words are. God loves each and every one of us. Each and EVERY ONE! It is so hurtful to watch your child struggle because of self righteous, ignorant behavior from someone, or even a group that has no idea what goes on outside of their narrow, little egocentric minds. Yes, I am very passionate about this, because not only is my child affected by those memes on social media that tell gay people they are sinning and going to hell. There are beatings and killings that cause them to live in fear. I know many wonderful, loving, compassionate souls who are gay, beautifully intertwined all through my life. Much like a rainbow, they add color to my days and light me up with loving words.

We are only as good as we treat others. We are called to love and that love has to be pure, God love. To be nice to someone's face, and then to turn around and talk behind their back about what sinners they are—well, they may not hear, but God does. God hears it before it even comes out of their mouths. God knows what's in our hearts. He knows our thoughts. He knows our intent, and He knows where we place our value by the way we treat others who may be different from us. Those who utter phrases such as, "Hate the sin, love the sinner," fail to see that what is being called the "sin" and the "sinner" are one and the same.

Scripture has been twisted so much that trying to find what the truth actually is, is like trying to escape through a labyrinth. Instead of finding fault in another lifestyle and in personal choices, look at yourself and find justice in how you live your life and leave the judging of others' souls to God. If you are offended by someone's lifestyle, look away, but don't think your life has been so perfect that you get to play judge and jury. There is enough hate in this world that those of us who strive to live in the Light are praying and have hope that bigotry and ignorance will be replaced with hearts that are inclusive and enlightened.

Archangel Sandalphon helped me write this section. Yes, an Archangel. So please understand that they love ALL as well.

I'll get down off my soapbox now.

I love this Bible verse: "There is no fear in love, but perfect love casts out fear. For fear has to do with punishment, and whoever fears has not been perfected in love." (1 John 4:18)

It's powerful Scripture that reminds us that love and fear cannot reside in the same heart. Stop and meditate on the love—the unconditional love that Source has for just you, a speck in this massive universe. Let it sink in.

Humbling, don't you agree? If you are cared for so much, then what is there to fear? If you believe in that unconditional love, fear will have no choice but to leave you. This is especially true when we are extending heart space to another person or when we share kindness with a stranger. Such acts of love show the true power within you that emanates from Source energy. It is embodied in the thought that we are so much more than our human bodies. We are a key component of this world and to the universe as a whole. Our life, our story, and how we tell and share it with another, is what expresses just how divine our lives are—how every breath we take is a part of the journey. It is a journey not just for us, but for the entire cosmos to expand and take shape for what lies beyond the lifetime we currently are living.

I was at my now ex-boyfriend's house during the night of a new moon. His house is out in the country where it's pretty dark and the stars are bright, which makes it easy to see planets and the constellations. It's actually quite stunning, and so I was always the dorky one who wanted to go outside and look at those stars and constellations. For whatever reason, when I look up at the night sky, it always feels like a piece of me is up there—like that's my home.

That particular night, I went out and laid down—no blanket or towel. I just laid on the asphalt driveway and became mesmerized by the vastness above me. My then boyfriend walked outside and said, "What are you doing laying on the ground like that?"

I asked him to come and lie down next to me, and he obliged. I began talking about the vastness, and the stars, and the beauty of the creation of space—the perfection of it all. And you have to realize, all we can see is a small part of the universe. An almost infinite number of galaxies exist that we cannot see.

I was thinking out loud and wondering if there are other planets in other galaxies that are like earth. I know ours is the central sun, but how many other suns and moons are there? Is there any way for science to possibly know that? Are we the only human life? Certainly, extra-terrestrials must exist somewhere. How incredibly deep, how wide and how vast the cosmos must be. The number of stars is practically infinite, yet Source "knows each one of them and calls them by name."

We are earthly stars, and to Source, we shine—we are important. To Source, we are unique in every way. Source sees us each as a perfect creation. Source knows every leaf on a tree and every hair on your head. If you think of how much love there is for each of us—even for the little bee that pollinates the flowers—and the flowers, too, are loved.

It's mind blowing that everything we do—lifetime after lifetime after lifetime—is documented. It's mind blowing that we are so infinitely loved, and that our souls are given multiple opportunities to "get it right." We are given the chance to become enlightened with every incarnation on this earth. That's why we're here. It's our soul's primary purpose. We are here to ascend, spiritually. We are here to heal wounds, to learn lessons and to recognize that divinity, Source, lives within and animates us. We are loved so much, we are afforded as many opportunities we need until we reach the ultimate goal. How beautiful of a love is that?

When we think of the beauty in everything that surrounds us, everywhere, not just in the area where we exist, how can we be afraid to express and return the infinite amount of love the universe has for us? Why should we fear what someone else thinks of us? How can we see ourselves as anything but perfection? How can we judge ourselves or others in any way?

Getting past the need to judge someone else is the first step to take when healing your own inner judgments. I don't think that fearing how someone is going to accept you or your ideals is what's at issue. I think it's the fear of how you will judge yourself if you feel you aren't accepted. The lack of belief in who you are will keep you from achieving what you came here to do. You have contracts with Source and other souls that you agreed to before you were born, and when you are fearful to reach out and show the world who you really are, it keeps you locked in a box, unable to satisfy those contracts. We have many opportunities to reach out and lend a helping hand to a stranger, but we just keep walking or driving out of fear.

I'm not saying to put yourself in unsafe conditions. We must be discerning of people and situations, and that discernment comes from our gut—our intuition. Sometimes that means picking up the phone and calling the police to assist someone in need of help, and sometimes it's a prayer.

Nelson Mandela once said, "I learned courage was not the absence of fear, but the triumph over it." It's true. When we step out in faith knowing that we are infinite beings at one with an infinite God, how can we not believe in our abilities to create our own internal and external worlds as we choose? Why do we feel limited in any way to change the world? For example, many politicians and preachers are able to create scenarios people accept as true because they possess the innate belief in themselves that they have the power to do so. They know they were created for greatness and whether you agree with the political position or the preaching, they are the movers and shakers whose ideas and actions carry weight. If we all had the same tenacity, belief and drive to create or change our lives, the world would be a better place because there'd be less poverty, less hunger, and less want.

Believe you can create your own reality, feel the energy and hold that feeling. Then follow your internal guidance and take inspired action. Truly, that is all there is to it. Find your power, believe it is there and don't you dare be fearful about living your own truth. Don't be fearful of judgment. Some of this world's famous inventors and scientists didn't allow naysayers or rude comments to stop them. They kept pushing, and because of that, we have electricity and telephones and all kinds of convenient devices at our fingertips. It happened because their belief was stronger than the ignorance that confronted them.

Our minds are super computers that have the ability to create cities, high rises and rocket ships. We are endowed with the ability of critical thinking that enables us to find solutions to serious problems or simple problems. Our minds can solve math equations, enable us to speak and inspire us to create. We breathe without thought and our internal organs function without us having to do anything.

Many do not realize it, but we also have a sixth sense that can open up an entire world beyond this physical reality. One of the most amazing things that our minds and the mind we all share create are synchronicities—meaningful coincidences. In addition, most people don't realize that our angels and guides are communicating with us through numbers, videos or commercials that pop up.

Our minds are wonderful but they can also be the human race's biggest problem. The fear minds create holds us back from achieving what we came here to achieve. We overthink and with that overthinking we find reasons why we can't, won't, or shouldn't. This is why it's important to find and walk the path of our very own Truth. Living in Truth and being truthful in all things is purity to Source. Doing so creates an allowing that opens the door to living a life in line with our soul's purpose. We all share the purpose of elevating the frequency of love in this world in order to build the bridge from the head to the heart, and then to one another.

Chapter Five

Walk In Your Truth

When I was doing research on the subject of living in one's truth, I came across so many different ideals, but mostly arguments between religions about who is wrong or right on the subject. Christians believe walking in truth is walking in the Truth of Jesus, as in 2 John 1:4-6, His life, death and resurrection. Other religions believe walking in truth is walking alongside your creator knowing you are supported in your life, so that you can live the truth of who you are.

I definitely believe in walking with Jesus, and I also believe we need to be intertwined with Source as we go along. We are guided to walk in our own beliefs, desires and to do so confidently in who we are and what we were created to do during our time on earth.

Some people get so consumed about being right about their position concerning their beliefs that they forget the simple fact that not everyone thinks the same way they do. They also forget, or perhaps they don't know that God, aka Source, does not want us to be in conflict with each other—that we are called only to love one another. Just as each of us wants to live what we believe or perceive to be true, so it is with others. No one likes to be told what to do or how to live, and when you try to force your views on another because you believe your religious dogma is the only truth, others are going to scatter like dust in the wind.

Just as we all want to be our authentic selves, we must allow our friends, relatives and strangers to do the same.

It actually doesn't take much effort to listen to someone speak their beliefs or what they think is true and simply withhold judgment. If you disagree, it is so much more respectful simply to say, "I appreciate your point of view. Thank you for sharing." Stay in peace, find your joy and stand in love. When people argue about who is right, no one wins. What results are two losers who are ticked off at each other.

At one time or another most of us have tried to interject our opinions onto someone else and force them to believe what we believe. My advice is to allow and accept differences. This is the way to be a bridge and show respect, which is a form of love. I believe that is what a true relationship with The Divine requires.

For many years I did not live my truth. I felt as if I had to cover up who I truly was to appease those people in my life, people I was sure would judge me. That caused me to become confused because my true nature pulled me in the direction I wanted to go, but what others expected of me pulled me to be a people pleaser. I would actually dumb myself down so other people would like me. That was tough, because I enjoy thought, introspection and asking questions.

I have always enjoyed learning about the "spiritual realm," but I was taught and therefore believed there was a demonic aspect to it that should never be channeled. All that changed after my healing and awakening. I was no longer asleep to my true nature. I fell in love with my truth—the real me. I felt Source calling on me to do so.

Source created who I am—even those things some folks might look down on me for. The truth is, we all have what might be called "shadows" within us. Some hide them better than others, and some of us parade them out on the front porch for the world to see. I prefer to hang out on the front porch, myself. Those are the real people not hiding anything and proud of who they are—the honest ones that know what is done in the dark is always brought out into the light.

When Source calls on you to grow, move forward, change and become, you cannot hold onto things, places or people who are stagnant. You can't hold onto anyone or anything that will hold you back. You can continue to love and help others, but your soul needs to move ahead and BECOME. That's what life should be about—becoming. We are all whole as we are, but when you feel there is more, that means that there is more and you ought to pursue it because we are here to grow.

All of this came to me when I was in spiritual solitude. I was living life, just doing my thing and Source started shaking me like a snow globe, because it was my time to evolve into who I am now and leave behind everything. And when I say everything, I mean everything. I felt the shift coming on for about six months. I noticed circumstances were shifting and people were changing or leaving. But going through day to day, it just seems like changes, speed bumps and flow. I went through my journal and created a timeline of everything that has shifted in my world. When I did that, I could see how each circumstance that should have felt traumatic was part of a divine path I had to follow in order to go through healing, awakening and begin on the journey of my calling.

It pretty much went into it full force when my daughter and I were living together in an apartment, splitting the bills. We did this for two and a half years. Then she came to me and said she and her partner were moving to another state. I'd never lived alone—ever. I had my oldest daughter when I was 16, and was married at age 20. I had my youngest daughter at 28. Even after I divorced, I lived with my daughter, or with friends. I'd had my own meal prep business for six years at that point, so I knew I could handle it financially. Or so I thought.

Six months before this happened, a friend from Florida came to live with us, so we moved from a two bedroom apartment to a three bedroom apartment that had a 13 month lease. That "friend" skipped out on us, and we had no idea where she went. So we were stuck paying more rent. Yet we were able to get our footing, so I purchased a new car on my own, which was divine timing. I'd been driving around in a 2001 Nissan Altima, which was a lousy car—it had 290,000 miles on it but it was still going. The upside was no car payment and cheap insurance!

One day, a client stopped by to pick up some food, and he asked when I was going to buy a new car. I said, "When the bumpers and tires fall off!" Five days later I was leaving a Publix parking lot and didn't see the yield sign, I ran into it with my passenger side bumper. I backed up and pulled out of the parking lot, dragging the bumper under my car. I got out, pulled it out and stuck it in the back seat. I was missing a third of the bumper, but I could still drive the car!

Then five days after that, I walked out of my apartment and I saw that I had a flat tire. My neighbor came over and helped me put the donut on it and I headed out to Walmart. I kid you not, I went into Walmart, came out with $426 worth of groceries, and guess what? That little donut was flat!

I called my daughter's girlfriend to come pick me up. I sat in that car waiting and heard, "It's time." I pulled up to Carvana and bought a car...

So there I was, paying extra rent, and now I had a car payment and more insurance. But I was still making ends meet.

When it was close to the time to move, my business slowed down—way, way down. I moved into a new apartment, and lo and behold, my business picked up for about eight weeks—then it completely tanked. I fell behind on my bills and had to call and make payment day adjustments. When all of this was going on, my dad was put in hospice care, which caused me to worry about my mom.

I was riding on the financial-struggle bus, my dad passed away, and a week later I broke up with my boyfriend. Strangely enough, however, I felt complete peace. I had so many cool synchronicities happen, which told me that everything was going to be okay.

This sense of solitude lasted for exactly 40 days—40 days! I started writing a book, then started over, then I started over again, and even with all of this going on, I knew it was all going to be okay. I was talking to my angels and I heard, "Google 'restaurant manager positions hiring near me.'"

I said, "I'm not getting back into the restaurant business!"

Well, I did the Google search and I was told to apply for the first and only position that came up. The next day I received a call from HR, went through three of the four interviews and was hired. I now believe Source was checking to see if I was going to be obedient and could handle with faith and grace what was being piled on top of me.

I passed the tests.

Through all of this I learned that living your truth is not about identifying with what you have accomplished. Instead, simply allow your soul to call you. In my time of solitude, I would sit in my apartment alone and talk to Source, angels, and my spirit guides. I never felt as though I was alone—not for a minute. I was more full of life than I had been in years. I was falling in love with Source, and with myself, all the while loving the process of alchemy. I was learning, reading and healing traumas—traumas that were my own, generational and ancestral. I was walking in nature with no earphones, no cell phone. I was listening to birds, to water rolling through the creek, and to squirrels chirping. I would notice hawks flying above—bluebirds, cardinals and mockingbirds flying around me. They would fly around my car as I drove along.

I have had so many experiences I could share that are other-worldly. Sometimes I would question if I was experiencing here-and-now reality. Of course, the spirit team around me let me know in subtle ways that I was not going insane.

I released the co-dependent relationship and the need for other people's approval. Nothing was more important to me than pleasing Source and being centered in who I am. It became clear that you can't live in truth and be codependent in relationships or hold onto any hate or animosity toward another. You have to take responsibility for your own feelings and emotions, and when you are entangled in an unhealthy relationship, you become consumed by it—you constantly feel upset or hateful because someone wronged you, and so you're playing a never ending blame game.

You can't get close to Source if you're living in negativity and your life is so consumed by another person or situation. There's no room for Source and there's no sense in trying to change. Truly, I tell you, what you need to do is step out in faith and take the steps needed to change yourself, and in doing so, your entire world. You have to cut the cord on things that no longer serve you. Otherwise, you will literally remain in a holding pattern of misery and regret. I wouldn't give back what I have gone through or take back any of those relationships pruned out of my life for anything. Where I am now is perfection, and I know what is there for me and that what is coming is everything I desire. Source will make good on those promises.

Here is a quote by Rumi, "Be the king who has made his own kingdom, be the moon who has made her own summit. How much longer will you coo-coo like a pigeon? Empty your head of all mortal lusts, and become life without breath. You will not call out for God any longer, for you have become immersed in God."

How beautifully are those words strung together? There had been so many times and years in my life, I would cry out to God, pleading to change my circumstances. In such times you feel as though you are pinched off. You can't feel the peace, so you go to the only place you know, and that is on your knees. If you go to Source daily and look for guidance in all the things you do, you will never need to cry out again, because your peace and answers will lie within you.

Our soul's desire is to live authentically and on purpose. It calls us to be the king of our own kingdom or queen of our own queendom. It starts by being independent of the opinions of others. The only opinion of you that counts, is the opinion you have of yourself. Let go of the desires of the world and live life in a way that's true to yourself—one dedicated to God for divine use. Be of service Source because there's nothing that feels better than the immersion in God that Rumi spoke of. Once you live your life of service to The Most High, you will have a deep desire to serve those around you with no thought of self, but rather, to serve with the peace and love that envelops you. No amount of worldly possessions can fill a void the way Source can. You will have an abundance of what truly matters on your soul's journey. You will be asked to trust in it and ask for it. Being at One with Source is like coming home to who you are. It is living in truth—living so abundantly, so authentically, you know everything you need is right there within you. Once I realized this was my truth and believed it, that everything I need is within me, I became free.

Source allows us to follow our own path in life. In our society most people want to attain a high level career position for monetary gain, they want the house, the nice car, the clothing, the lover and all of the tangible things the world has to offer and that's to be expected in today's cultural environment. But at some point, if that's what you focus on exclusively, you will miss Source. You'll attain your possessions, but in your heart you will begin to feel that there must be more to life. You'll be like Peggy Lee singing the old song, "Is that all there is?" That's when it's time to call on Source to show you the path to fulfillment.

I was talking to my oldest daughter, who has made a beautiful and successful life for herself, but she said she felt something inside was missing. She has built a million dollar business, is known in her field and teaches the business side of her craft. She has a beautiful family, and lives a life full of freedom. She has gone to church for years, given her time to the worship team, and she participates in Bible studies and women's groups. She has always had a heart that's seeking a relationship with God. But this particular night, she told me she felt called to do more. She felt confused and so tender-hearted. She knew she was being asked to move in a new direction, and with that came the fear she would not have the life she desires. How would she afford the things she wants?

I said to her, "What if what is on the other side of your obedience is better than what you have now? What if there is a better home in store for you than the one you're dreaming of, or can afford now?"

There are times we fill our lives by going through the motions, instead of just being, listening and allowing. Source was calling her to be and to allow—calling her away from doing all the "Christian" things, to crossing over and going deeper into the relationship.

After over a three hour phone call, she recognized the synchronicities that were guiding her, and calling her, but she questioned whether it might be her imagination, or if it really was God calling her. I could tell by the excitement in her voice that it was a God thing. I told her that Abraham Hicks says, "If it's God, it feels good." I asked her if she felt good and it was a resounding "Yes!"

What she feared was the unknown. That fear, as I have said, is what keeps us from our purpose or calling in life. All Source wants from us is to fully submit to doing what we came here on earth to do in this incarnation, and believe that we will be given the tools to get it done.

What I am trying to drive home is that when you search and you strive to live your life in spiritual peace, you are telling Source your body and mind are open to being used for divine purpose. You are allowing yourself to be an instrument through which Source's energy can flow.

Let me tell you about a Brazilian man named Mauricio Panisset, who is known as the "Man of Light." He had an incredible gift. Cosmic light would come through his physical body, and because of this he could be used as an instrument for Source to bring about mental, physical, emotional and spiritual healing to those people he touched.

He said, "When you are filled with love it pours out of you and into other people. It pours into every living thing. It pours into your work. When you trust in yourself, you trust in the wisdom that created you."

It's the trust and the belief of what can be done through you that will change the way you perceive yourself and your relationship with other people and Source. What changed me was finally feeling free to share my abilities to communicate with the other side. So I broke down the walls that separated me from God and allowed the pouring out of love to flow through. I trusted the process and opened up the gift I'd been given that could help heal and bring closure to those who'd had a loved one crossed over.

My nephew crossed over when he was only 20 years old. As you can imagine, it was devastating for our family. One day about a year after he crossed, I was sitting at my computer and I got very cold. The hair stood up on my arms, and I could feel a cold breeze next to my ear. I heard, "Hi Aunt Kimmy." It was his voice—he had come to see me. I treasured that, and it was one of the best experiences of my life.

One of the first people I opened up to about my ability was my ex boyfriend's, ex wife. I'll call her Sue, which is not her real name. I went to her house to deliver something to her, and when I got to her driveway, her mom, who'd passed away a few years before, was there. Sue's mom told me to ask about something brown with white flowers.

I said, "Really?" Then I realized that if I didn't use my gift when called upon, my ability to receive such messages would diminish. So, I knew I needed to share the message.

When I went in, I said, "Your mom is here and she's telling me about something brown with white flowers."

Sue had no idea what I was talking about, but said she was still going through her mom's things and said she would let me know if she found anything.

I never said anything to my ex boyfriend about it until about four months later. I was at Sue's house again delivering something, and I asked if she had found anything, and she hadn't. I left her house feeling like I must have been way off on that one—maybe I was out of practice, I wasn't sure. I went to my ex's house and when we were talking, I told him about what happened.

He said, "Hold up," and pulled a tan plate down that had brown trim and white flowers. His former mother-in-law had given it to him. The message had been for him!

Well, I began to channel for him, too. I was able to contact his dad. I brought them together, and some healing took place.

I was driven by those experiences, and I have to say that it was incredibly humbling to channel things that were just between them.

When I channel, I feel the energy. When I first channeled his dad the energy was good, but as they communicated, they both became jovial and at peace. Not only does this sort of thing heal those left behind, it gives those who have crossed over peace as well, and it gives them closure, too.

The first time I channeled my grandma, I was in the fetal position on the floor and wept. She was my favorite person—I love her so much. When she was still living, she was in California when I had moved to Illinois. She kept asking me to come to visit her one year for Christmas, but I couldn't work it out. I felt a lot of guilt about it, and when I learned she had crossed over just a little over a week after that Christmas, that guilt ballooned into pain. I held onto that guilt for years—until I started this journey. I'd felt her with me much of the time after she passed, but when I finally connected with her, she let me know she was not upset, and that she loved me. Well, it set me free.

In case you aren't aware, those who are now on the other side still carry the same personality, but they just don't have the ego they had on earth—all they know is love. That's it, pure love.

A neighbor girl who lived across the hall from me in my apartment complex and I were chatting and I said, "Do you have a loved one who crossed over the last couple of years, by the name of Emily."

She looked at me perplexed and said, "My grandma died two years ago from Covid, and her name was Emily."

I told her she was there with her, and that she wanted her to know of her love.

I have many stories I could tell of how these encounters bring healing to both sides. Your loved ones communicate with you in different ways. My ex, for example, would find coins in the most random places. His dad was a coin collector, and so his dad was using coins to let him know he was around. When you find certain things or come across little objects that remind you of them, that's probably what's going on—they're leaving you a treasure.

We're never alone. We are always surrounded with support and love. Just because you can't see what's there doesn't mean it isn't there. As God says, faith isn't seeing, it is knowing.

There are two categories of people: five sensory, non-spiritual people and multi-dimensional, spiritual people. Most are in the five-sensory category, but more people are experiencing an awakening journey because of the astrological age we now have moved into. A lot of people want to debate this, mostly because we are human and just about every human has an opinion. However, my intuition, plus how the spiritual environment feels to me indicates that we are currently in a period of transition. We actually did start into the age of Aquarius back in the 1960's.

An age lasts approximately 2,160 years. Our astrological calendar is currently muddied with the transition from Pisces into Aquarius, which produce two completely different energies. If you want to deep dive into this, it is amazing to see how much the world evolves during these times. The Age of Aquarius is going to be one that is bringing with it the opening of souls, peoples' eyes, minds and the evolution of the heart space. Even in a world of chaos, people are beginning to search for more understanding, and that includes more questions about what has been taught to us as a society.

A lot of people want answers. I believe that going within is how to find them. Typically, we try to put everyone in a one-size-fits-all box, and that doesn't work. When we open ourselves up to and ask Source, our angels and our spirit team, we receive answers that are meant specifically for us as individuals. In addition doing so helps form the personal and intimate relationship very much desired by Source. Your own consciousness, your soul, desires that as well.

The one thing I tell everyone who comes to me for advice or for help on their spiritual journey is to buy a journal and start writing. When I first started journaling it was about all of the "things" I was going to manifest, such as I'm going to get this, and I'm going to do all of these things. But over time it evolved into a relationship with Source. The bonus became all of the cool things that were being shown to me. I go back and read those journal entries knowing I have reached a higher level of spiritual maturity that continues to grow every day. It stopped being about how God can serve me, but rather, how I can serve God as well as other people. That's what growth is all about. What can I give of myself? How can I be of service?

Just start writing about of the things that you desire. Write what you want your life to look like and the things you want that are tangible—so much of the time, that's exactly where we need to begin. Figure out what motivates and excites you, then do what needs to be done. Manifesting is about raising your vibration to bring about the things that you desire—the comforts, the money, the business, the romantic partner. You have to vibrate higher, visualize and believe it is yours. Then you get to a point of growth and it becomes about raising your frequency to the required Source frequency.

Source already knows your heart—just put it on paper. I just did a full moon manifestation and wrote down the desires of my heart. I quit writing "I want" or "I will have" or "One day—" Instead, I began writing "I have" and "I am" or "It is" because it is my belief that it is all already mine and will come in perfect timing.

Write about what happened to you that day, such as the synchronicities you notice, the epiphanies that you received, the wisdom nuggets given to you. Those things are pure gold. Write the things you are releasing from your life. Share how you're feeling about a situation or a person. It's your journal and you are writing to the Universe. Do it your way.

One thing I do every single night, I write or say out loud what I call my "I am thankfuls." I date my journal and begin my entry with, "I am thankful for," and proceed to write what it is, and why I am thankful for it.

Having a conversation out loud or in a letter to Source or talking with your angels doesn't need to be formal. Just speak to and write how you would with anyone else in your life. They know everything about you, and love you just the way you are. They're your closet friends. I cut up with them when I write. It's like writing a note to my best friend because that is what they are. You don't need to say "thee" and "thou" because they are very hip to the current times. You just need to show up as you are and know you'll be accepted.

I also have a dream journal I keep next to my bed. I do astral travel as I sleep, and I also go into the Akashic Records. Journaling what you remember from dreams can help you piece together answers. Things may not make sense at that moment, but a few months down the road you'll remember something you wrote down from a dream or a download, and it will be the answer you were searching for at that very moment.

As I learned to walk in my own truth, gained trust in myself and my path, I was told that I'm a Chosen One—chosen to be a teacher and to help lead others to awaken on their path. I accepted the position offered by Source, and I'm here to tell you, if you're reading this book, you probably are a Chosen One, too. To arrive at that point, you need to get on your path and begin the process of healing. Once you get to the space of being comfortable living in your truth, the more divine work will be entrusted to you. That work is being Chosen to generate love in order to take another step on the bridge.

Chapter Six

Chosen One

I was instructed to write this chapter about being a Chosen One. It is one I would have said "no" to before, because it might seem as if I am inflating myself by sharing this. But the Archangels want it shared, because there are those of you who are reading this who are Chosen.

Not everyone will lay down their lives and follow in blind faith. How did I find out and come to the realization I am a Chosen One, that I'm here to work for Source? My answer is short and easy. I was told. Like everything else that has come to me on this journey, I am open to receive, and it was given to me very clearly. I had an Archangel come to visit me one night. I wasn't asleep, but rather, I was in deep meditation. I had my third eye open and could see how incredibly bright and beautiful this angel was. It was Archangel Michael, and he told me I was a Chosen One, and that when I needed to know where to go and when, I would be told. He said he would come to me and tell me. I agreed that I would listen and follow the guidance that would be given.

When you open yourself to belief that the spirit realm can speak to you directly, and have faith, it happens. When you live in consciousness, you live in what is referred to as "The Bardo," which is the "in-between" between physical and nonphysical reality. In other words, as a Chosen One, you live between the three-dimensional realm and the spirit realm, simultaneously. We can feel and see what's on the other side, but we are still living in human form. We are here in the 3-D realm to have the experiences that foster our soul's evolution. We're here to live in our truth for this incarnation. We're here to take what we gain with us when we progress into the next incarnation—if or when we choose to come back.

I went through a time where I was asking Source why I was chosen to share these messages. I am not worthy to represent the heavenly realm. I am not perfect. I am a sinner. I have made terrible choices in my life. Not only am I divorced, a myriad of decisions I made in my life certainly have not made me worthy of me being chosen.

I was reminded that the 12 disciples were not chosen because of their perfect lives. As a matter of what I believe is fact, and you may say is opinion, the 12 disciples were hand picked because they were not perfect. That's why they were chosen. Peter, the founder of the Church, for example, made a ton of mistakes. It was God's way of saying, you don't need to be perfect to be used for divine purpose, you simply need to be willing to lay down your life and surrender. My imperfect life is proof of this. My imperfect journey should communicate the message that no matter who, what, when, where, why or how you did your life, what you carry deep within your soul is what truly matters. I had to go through the life's lessons I have endured in order to be understanding and empathic to others. I had to live in the way I did, in a sinful nature, to develop an understanding of the flesh. The perfect unfolding of then to now and years to come, is a message that Source wants me to share.

Source said to me, "I need you to rise up and fill your role. You are a spark to ignite the fire in others. This is more than just who you are, this is leading and teaching others so they too can live in their roles and fulfill their divine purposes."

We are living in such a pivotal time of awakening. Most can feel the divine shift happening, but are unaware of what's going on. This is why to most people it feels like chaos, and yet those who understand what is happening are more at ease. They are waiting in expectation.

We are so accustomed to living in a tangible world that this shift of collective consciousness on our planet will have many people feeling as if they are living in total confusion. Over time, however, your soul will adapt your mind and physical body to these changes, and things will settle down and smooth out.

Most people who know that they are Chosen have the same life experiences. So much so, that when you research the topic, it all lines up.

I want to share with you ten different aspects of a life as someone who is Chosen. It is usually most of these signs you have experienced, not just a few, but most to all. Personally, I have experienced all of these:

1. You are the "black sheep." You never quite fit in, anywhere. This is the one I have felt the most. I would be in a group of people and never feel as though I fully belonged. I never felt as if I meshed completely, and it wasn't for lack of trying. Many times I have been out at a party and found myself sitting alone because that is

where I feel most comfortable. I have only experienced a handful of close relationships. Most of my life, I didn't even feel like I fit into my own family. I feel the most at ease with my children. They know me and love me and they are who I trust the most. When I speak to other Chosen (yes, I feel the energy and my intuition tells me when I am around someone with a special mission), trust is the aspect that is at the top of the list. I have a deep sense of knowing when someone does or doesn't like me, or who likes to turn others against me with untruths or slander, and because of this, I keep myself at a distance. When I have gone against my intuition and tried to make someone like me, it always back-fired. It usually results in the heated coals of the fire of disdain coming towards me. I now know that this was a protection of Source to keep me out of the inner circle of those I'm not intended to have in my life.

2. You may have experienced many traumas in your lifetime. Your childhood could have been tumultuous. Your life just never seemed to flow, and if it did, it was short lived. It could have been one thing after another, and feeling as if you just needed a break from life. My entire life has been this way. Because of my life in general and my own bad choices, I never felt like I was living a remotely "normal" life. I can look back on ALL of it now and know that it was the divine plan to get me to where I am today. I may

have taken many side roads and unnecessary detours, but I have ended up where I am supposed to be. I know many of those who are Chosen have been abused in some way—financial struggles that always surface and parents who may have been alcoholics, drug addicts or emotionally distant. This forces us to have to heal the childhood wounds, and many times, it opens us up to breaking those generational curses.

You have moved a lot and questioned everything. I have moved so many times in my life—I can't even remember where or how many homes or apartments. I've lived in California, Kansas, Illinois, Florida, Kentucky and Tennessee. All in each state, there were multiple homes. I never grew any roots, and I'm not even sure if where I am now is where I'll spend my life. Many times this is because, along your life's path you are supposed to touch lives with your Light that you aren't even aware you have. You never really fit in, so you don't feel like you have an affect on anyone, but you do. Now that I am awakened, I realize that because I know so many people from all over the country and other parts of the world, my message has a far reach. This has opened my eyes as to why I had to live in so many places. I have also questioned everything in my life and one of the reasons why I am writing this book is that I began to question the beliefs I had. These were the beliefs I'd inherited and never questioned. I realized I had beliefs, but I lacked a relationship with Spirit. Many of us go through the motions, never challenging what we are taught, and yet we should. We come from an old school way of thinking and yet I know it is time to embrace more love and compassion to include everyone. In generations past, the Germans killed the Jews. Black people were killed because they were considered dispensable. Women who were considered witches were hanged, drowned, or burned at the stake because they had cats and made herbal medicine. Gays were treated unjustly because of their lifestyles. I have always asked "why" in life. I was never fully at ease with things at face value and this caused me to dive deeper into subjects and learn. Back in those very few instances I mentioned, people believed they were doing the right things. They even created laws to enforce their bigotry and hatred. Question everything, especially if you are Chosen.

3. You tend to walk alone in life and enjoy your solitude. I like to be in my own company. I didn't realize this until I went into spiritual solitude. There is a stigma that follows those who choose to be by themselves—we get judged. When I've told people I like to be alone to think, I have been called a "serial killer." The 40 days when I had very little contact with other humans was fine with me. I find myself to be hilarious, and I communicate with the other side—where I do feel as if I fit in completely—

and so I never feel alone. The human circle of family and friends I do have, I keep small. I prefer to listen to people I'm not close with. I don't share a lot of who I am, but will share, when guided, any message my angels and guides are telling me to share. People who are Chosen know they have to cheer for themselves. You find that people don't like you for what seems like no reason, and you feel like an outcast. I had the intuitive hit one day that told me it was because those that live in the dark are triggered by your Light. Living in the dark, doesn't mean someone is evil, it means that they are very much living in their carnal or human nature. When you cast your light, it makes them not like you. Take it as a compliment as I now do. When I realize that someone excludes me from things because they don't like me, I know that they don't like my light and I am thankful I no longer feel the need to go along with things to try to fit in. I'm comfortable just being me, as should you.

4. You follow your own heart, because authenticity is your compass. Yes, you generally pick the road less traveled. Most people find a job and stay with it for years, even if they're miserable. I just never put up with anyone's grap and would move on. I have always enjoyed working for myself and being my own person, making my own hours and have believed the wind would blow me in the right direction, or that

God would show me the way. You're living your life and there's always this nagging feeling that you have a mission here on earth. You know that you're here for more than what's on the surface. You're here to create change. Maybe you're here to build bridges that spread love and compassion to all people. One day you're just doing your thing and the next day Source begins your process of awakening. I always felt that my purpose was greater than the life I was living. When my soul's calling was finally revealed to me, I realized why I was never satisfied being in one place very long, and that goes for a job or where I lived. It was me being restless, but not knowing why. When you finally realize what your direction is, you are at peace right where you are and live in expectation that Source will guide you every step of the way. When you live a life that is authentic to who you are, you become a beacon—one who makes the journey easier for others to follow.

6. You have lived many lives in your lifetime. This knits together many of the other aspects of your journey. Moving a lot, never fitting in, job hopping, feeling restless. You may have done a lot of different things, worn many hats and always done a great job at each of them. I've always been pretty fearless when it came to trying new jobs, but somehow I always did well or excelled at whatever I've done. I have had so many experiences in my life. From bagging groceries

to getting a product I made into Whole Foods and other smaller grocery chains. I've run my own businesses, but I have also been in executive level positions with restaurants and a cosmetics company. I've even delivered mail, which was not my favorite job, but I did it!

7. You have a deep reverence for the spirit world and do not feel as if you are part of this physical world. You feel as if there is more than this life. There have been times I have looked up at the night sky and felt that was where I needed and wanted to be. You get to a point in your life where you just decide to be genuine and you don't want to deal with the fakeness of this world. The connections you desire are first and foremost—with Source and working with your spirit team to bring about the changes you were sent here to be a part of. You know your human job is on this earth, but your soul knows that it is part of the collective consciousness. The connection I have with the spirit world is deep, and it deepens more every day. I also have days that I don't feel it as much, but I know my frequency is still lined up and I am being guided on my path.
8. Your internal world seems to begin to change and your soul begins to lead you to where your Light is supposed to be. When this happens you begin to trust your gut without question and become willing to take risks, to own your decisions and to prioritize. As your internal world changes, so does the world around you. You be-

come more sensitive to what is on television, to music and to the energy of places and people. You become picky as you choose the things you digest through your eyes and ears, because just like food, these things will have a positive or negative impact on your internal self and spiritual sphere. You become highly-sensitive to everything around you. Once I spent an entire Saturday being fully connected and deep in meditation—all day long. I went to the store the next day, and when I walked in, I felt as if I had this gold bubble around me. As people walked by, they looked dead in the eyes. There was no love flowing out of them. When a woman walked by me that was smiling and glowing, it was like we recognized the light within each other. I felt as though Source surrounded me with that bubble to protect my precious energy. There have been numerous times since then that I have been encapsulated by the gold bubble. All I have to do is ask for it, and it is done. It can be so for you, too. You just need to get connected to Spirit and be open to being used as a light and an instrument for love.

9. You are giving, compassionate, selfless and a helper. There was a point in my life I had enough of being the doormat. I vowed to never help another person because I was tired of being crapped upon. But that just isn't my nature. I think what changed for me was that I learned to be a giver and a helper, but with clear

and helpful boundaries. When you are a true empath—and I hear people throwing that word around without truly understanding what it is—your heart hurts when someone around you is hurting. If you don't create healthy boundaries, you can be taken advantage of. Boundaries are important. They will protect you from a lot of negative emotions that may well up in you, or be pointed in your direction from another person. The gift of loving compassion comes straight from Source and should be given with a servant's heart—never with the intent of personal gain. Being a selfless person is exactly what we need to be, but we do need to be selfish about protecting our energy and interests at all times. When we show the right level of balance and maturity, the Universe will continue to give us opportunities to serve others and allow the opening of love and compassion to flow back to us.

10. You have a desire to lay down your life to serve Source and humanity. Until I understood this completely, and I mean in absolute terms, I did not have the correct idea of what this meant. We have all heard the saying, "God first, spouse second, family third." In reality, we have no idea what that means. We go to church and claim to put God first, when we actually do not. Let me explain. Once you reach that depth of connection, where you are willing, when asked, to walk away from any relationship, any amount of money and any possession in order to follow

The Divine when prompted, you know what laying down your life really means. When I gave up the dead end relationships, bad habits and carnal lifestyle to follow the path Source had for me, when I was willing to be healed, guided, molded, refined by the fire and compressed into the diamond I have become, I felt every emotion and passion of what it means. When your life becomes the desire to put the requests of Source miles ahead of what you or anyone wants of you, you have laid down your life. I know that what is meant for me will come along in the perfect timing, and I won't need to question it. My work, my family, my love relationship and my passions will all flow and become as Source guides. To lay down your life isn't about not having things, or not living, it is about leaving behind what you want and allowing Source to guide you to what's best for you. We only want what we think we can attain one day, but Source has dreams and plans for us that we think we can't reach. But we can attain them if we set aside our own desires to do divine works for Source and humanity. Jesus said, "Lay down your life and follow me." This means, lay down your human desires and your soul will be open to the promptings that show you the way along your path. Follow in compassion, love, joy and peace and Source will fill your cup daily.

I have a list written of different stories, anecdotes and quotes for this chapter, and I was just visited by Archangel Gabriel to include Pope Francis, head of the Catholic Church, the bishop of Rome and sovereign of the Vatican City State. I know absolutely nothing about the Catholic Church. I don't turn on the television, don't watch news, and I haven't been on social media for quite some time. So, what I am about to share came as quite a shock to me, but it was also a very cool experience! I learned that the Pope and I are speaking the same language and guided by Source about being the bridge between religions, cultures, races and lifestyles. Here's how it went down. I was in the bathtub having a conversation with my angels about what I should write beyond what I have already listed. Next thing I knew I was being told, "Mother Teresa," and I was completely confused. Then Archangel Gabriel told me to get my Emerald Tablets book and turn to page 40. I was instructed to read T4 V11 which is, "Forth then, my soul sped throughout the cosmos, seeing ever new things and old; learning that man is truly space-born, a Sun of the Sun, a child of the Stars."

So I asked what that meant and why it was what I received as a message. You need to understand, I am still in complete awe about this, but I was told to share it. Pope Francis is a child of the Stars and a Chosen One they want included in this chapter. They want it said that he has been incarnated here to be a pillar and teacher of peace. As I researched his teachings, I was shocked that much of what I journaled over the years was the same as the teachings of Pope Francis. One of his quotes, "Dialogue is born from an attitude of respect for another person, from a conviction that the other person had something good to say. It assumes that there is room in the heart for the person's point of view, opinion, and proposal. Dialogue entails a cordial reception, not a prior condemnation. To dialogue it is necessary to know how to lower defenses, open the door of the house, and offer human warmth."

Pope Francis has promoted interfaith ceremonies, bringing together the Jewish, Muslim, Evangelical and Orthodox Christian faiths to pray for a peaceful solution to the Middle East Conflicts. Shortly after he was elected, he called for more inter-religious dialogue as a way of "building bridges" and establishing "true links of friendship between all people." He said that his title of "pontiff" means "builder of bridges," and that it was his wish that "the dialogue between us should help to build bridges connecting all people, in such a way that everyone can see in the other not an enemy, not a rival, but a brother or sister to be welcomed and embraced."

He has also said of non-believers when responding to a list of questions published in a newspaper, "You ask if the God of Christians forgives those who do not believe and who do not seek faith. Given the premise, and this is fundamental, that the mercy of God is limitless for those who turn to him with a sincere and contrite heart, the issue for the unbeliever lies in the obeying of his or her own conscience."

He says of atheists, "[Jesus] has redeemed us all, all of us, with the Blood of Christ: not just Catholics. Everyone! Even the atheists. Everyone!"

In 2013, when he was speaking about the LGBTQ community, he stated, "The key is for the church to welcome, not exclude, and show mercy, not condemnation."

Something I am very passionate about, because I have a daughter who is gay, are children who are homeless because their parents threw them out of their homes—because they came out of the closet. It is my goal to build group homes for these kids to go to. All children need to feel compassion, love, grace and kindness.

One quote by Pope Francis that hit my heart was, "We have to find a way to help that father or mother to stand by their [LGBTQ] son or daughter." How can a parent turn his or her back on a child because of who that child is?

This needs to change and a pouring out of love needs to happen—society needs to be inclusive of everyone. I have been told that Pope Francis is here to also bring the Truth about the love and the longing there exists for each of us to find our way back home to Source. I had no knowledge of this before this evening, but I am so thankful to know that I am in agreement with and can stand side by side with Pope Francis to bring the message that everyone has a place and a purpose in this world—as well as a home in the heavenly realms. We may not see things the same way on every issue, but we do on what Source feels is one of the most important conversations we all need to have about unity and loving each other. It is my hope that I can bring about the same positive aspects of love and acceptance Pope Francis has shared in his life. We should all live this message daily.

The one person I have looked to because of his teachings is Dr. Wayne Dyer. He says, "Don't die with your music still inside you." This powerful phrase simply means, don't allow yourself to live any life other than the one you were born to live.

When you are a Chosen One, you have a Divine purpose that is going to change the world. It may be after your death, but it will change the course of humanity. We have a big job, and once you are called to open your eyes to it, and you open your heart to do the work, you need to lay everything down in order to follow Source and lead others to continue the shift into our new world of abundant love.

There have been times when I was shown the past of my present life and that of several past lives. While watching them—what seemed like movies in my mind's eye—it seemed like a symphony. It all flowed in perfect harmony from the past up to the moment I am in now.

If we don't get our soul's purpose accomplished in this life, we will continue to incarnate until it is fulfilled. Realize, you will come back until you get your contracts signed, sealed and delivered. This is why living your life in a way that serves Source is how you will live a life with the music flowing through you and out of you. It is music the orchestra of life creates as you fulfill your purpose. Allow yourself to see what is showing up for you, including what seem to be challenges. It is when we are being challenged or tested, that we grow the most. If we embrace the obstacles we face, allow and accept the messages they bring us, learn from and grow in our spiritual walk as a result, we will achieve what we were sent here to do.

If you feel as if you aren't a Chosen One in this lifetime, you may be in the next or in another one after that. This isn't a race. Everything is already in motion. The Universe knows exactly the players it needs when it needs them.

Your soul has as its divine purpose what it needs to learn now, and all of the teachings you have had in all of your lives will be there for you when you need them.

As mentioned above, I was shown who I was in my past life and what has carried over into this one. I had no idea who the person was, but once it was revealed, and I learned about that life, I realized I am continuing the job that my soul had in that one. I will share this in another chapter. I have been shown numerous lives through the Akashic records and what the Archangels have shared with me in order to give me the courage to write this book. I am educated and worthy of writing and teaching in this life. My soul's journey has earned it.

Surrender and the doors will open.

Chapter Seven

Gratitude and Surrender

I want to learn to think like God thinks.
—Albert Einstein

We're likely to become cynical if we think we are separate from God, and cynicism makes it impossible to build bridges of love, compassion and acceptance. The truth, however, is that Source not only loves, but is in all creation, including you. You are an extension of Source, and when you know that, truly internalize it, you cannot have a thought against any person or thing.

As His representative on Earth, you begin to think like God. You know that what's happening at this moment is supposed to happen, and so you let go of the urge to judge. You accept and love all people, no matter their race, religion, beliefs or lifestyle. You accept others and allow them to live their personal truth. You possess and acknowledge the flame of love God has placed in each of us—love you feel for yourself as well as others because you understand you must love yourself to truly love anyone else. Doing so is true surrender, and you know and show gratitude as a result.

One journal entry I made and believe all of us should take time to write is, "Ten Things That Are WONDERFUL About Me."

This is not to be vain, shallow or full of yourself. It is to acknowledge who you are. There's nothing wrong with being kind to the beautiful being that is you. Believe in the goodness you bring into this world and carry that with you every day. Feel gratitude for who you are and surrender to who truly you are.

Here are my Ten:

1. I can bring light and joy into a room.
2. I speak to people's truths and help them see the bigger picture of who they really are. I help them see their greatness.
3. I am giving of my time and resources.
4. I love to serve others, and I am kind.
5. I love who I am. All the time. No matter what.
6. I am always thankful and grateful.
7. I am intelligent and beautiful.
8. I enjoy making others feel welcomed and included.
9. I am healed and humbled.
10. I am an incredible child of The Most High. I am a beautiful Lightworker. I am a Chosen One, who will be teaching others to live in the Light. I will assist others, working with Source, to bring about the new world of love, kindness and compassion. I have a deep and profound purpose in this life.

Whatever you believe you are, you are correct. Because your thoughts are what bring about your truth. The good news is that we are allowed to change our minds and get ourselves up out of the pit of limited thinking and thereby rid ourselves of lower vibrational beliefs. Be the alchemist who creates the change needed to live big and on purpose in your calling in order to follow your heart.

Ram Dass said, "A lot of our problem comes from our inability to accept our own beauty and accept the grace that comes into our life."

Unfortunately, we are often taught at home and in school that we are less than we are. We are taught that we need to be humble, and in order to be humble we can't see ourselves the way God sees us. And God is going, "Heyyyy! It's okay to think good things about who you are, and to accept a compliment when someone else sees goodness in you!"

You must love who you are first, then love others, and when you do, the love for life will follow. Awaken your sense of gratitude for all things, yourself included. What Source truly loves, is when you are grateful for everything big or small that you receive. If you find a penny on the ground, pick it up and thank Source for that penny. It isn't about the value. It's about having gratitude in your heart for all things. The more we are grateful for what we might consider small things, the more big things will show up for us.

The Buddhists take a bite of food, lay their down the utensil and meditate on that bite as they chew. They do not pick up the fork until that food is completely chewed and swallowed. That is how they show gratitude for the food they eat.

Be grateful you can walk because there are those who have legs that don't work. Be grateful for your home—there are those who are homeless. Be grateful for the love of your partner in life because there are those who have had one cross over, or who dream of a life with someone to love who will love them in return. Be thankful for your solitude for this is when you can hear the answers to your prayers that come from the spirit realm. Be grateful for running water and electricity—many countries do not have that. We are so very blessed to be clothed, fed and educated. We are free to be who we are and free to choose the life we want to live. It is time to stop walking through life like a zombie, or in judgment, and to find joy because you are grateful for life itself.

On the beautiful journey I've been on, and even more so on my spiritual journey, my eyes have been opened to be appreciative of everything—even what I viewed as trying times or difficult challenges. I now embrace the challenges because I know that getting through them by surrendering to the process with a sense of gratitude is elevating me to new levels of understanding.

Before I awakened, I believed that the world was against me. I would brood about how unfair life is and would take on a "why-me" mentality. That way of thinking never served me because the more I focused on the negative, the more negative stuff I received. Doesn't it seem as though when one thing goes wrong, something else negative is likely to follow?

During the beginning of my spiritual awakening, I was listening to Abraham Hicks, and what was said woke me up to how my thoughts created my emotions and how my emotions and feelings created my reality. Truly the Law of Assumption is always at work, and depending on our mental attitude, it can create a chain of negative events. The Law of Assumption is simply that what you assume will happen is likely to happen. If you assume that something bad is going to come along, it will. What you assume becomes a never-ending cycle. I have always assumed people didn't want to be around me, that people didn't like me and that every situation would end badly for me. And because of that, I created a negative reality that hung over my head.

Now I assume the opposite, and I don't really care how anyone feels about me. I know Source loves me. I love me and that the people that are important in my life also love me. My new assumption is that whatever I am experiencing at this present moment is happening to teach me something new. It may be to prompt me to take the correct path, or to help me progress toward my life's calling.

Here's an example of how I used to think that kept me in a negative cycle. It's an example of how my thinking has changed about situations that in the past would have triggered negative outcomes. In jobs I've had as a manager or supervisor of others, I would get involved in whatever drama was taking place. I would feel hurt when people didn't like me, or if they ignored me, and then I would allow myself to become uncomfortable with the job. I'd end up quitting because I allowed what I believed to be reality to dictate my emotions. This about-face has changed my reality.

In my current position as a restaurant manager, I am going through training with a girl who is 22 years younger than I am, and the training manager is just a few years older than she is. Because they are of the same generation, they immediately hit it off. Both project the personality trait, "I am woman hear me roar," and call themselves "black cats" that have men who are like "labrador retrievers" in their lives. They consider themselves badass women who don't get pushed around because of their toughness.

I was the same sort of person most of my life. I thought I had to prove myself by pumping myself up with my words. At times, I carried myself in a way that made me seem unapproachable at work because I believed that was how you got respect.

I now realize that attitude just made me seem like a bitter bitch, and if people didn't like me, it was because of the persona I thought I needed to carry. At my age now, and where I am in my spiritual walk, I don't need to "roar." Now I look at myself, not as a black cat, but as a lion. A lion doesn't need to do anything except to just be and allow. A lion has a quiet confidence, and it receives respect from the environment that surrounds it because it is the king or queen of its own world. But if that lion does need to roar, it will, and it gets its point across justly and firmly without any casualties along the way.

The lion has a presence that indicates it's in control of itself and can control any situation that comes along. I lie in the quiet confidence of Source energy and that is my power, that is my "roar." In the past I would have seen these two women getting along, becoming friends, and would have taken it personally. Now, I just don't care. I realize I don't want to be friends with everyone, and that I am not everyone's cup of tea. I am there to do the best job I can and to show other people love and compassion. I am a Light in what is normally considered a hectic, draining and drama-filled workplace. I know it is not the place where I am going to spend the rest of my life. I know Source has my path laid out before me, and I will be given the opportunity to achieve the goals and dreams I desire. I know my life is one that is of the Divine, and where I am now is on a path to where I am going. I also know this job is teaching me so much about myself. I'm learning how to deal with all of the different personalities surrounding me, and I can see how I've grown.

In a short period of time, Source has shown me just how powerful I am, that with my courageous voice I can shift timelines to make necessary changes around me and the collective. I know it is best to sit back, watch and listen—that it is best not to take part in situations in which I don't have a positive role to play. When you give yourself over to Source, you realize your importance is of a spiritual nature, and getting involved in worldly ego-driven drama is not something to be part of. If gossip begins, for example, I walk away without explanation.

There is power in not feeling a need to fit in. I have given up the idea that the challenges you face are supposed to break you, and now realize they are put in your path so you can learn from them, and thereby create a new version of yourself. Once you accept this, you will find the lessons move through your reality at a quick pace, and that circumstances soon fall into place. It's acting upon emotions generated by your ego, and ignoring the lesson being delivered by a situation that keeps you stuck in what can become a never-ending cycle of turmoil and stress.

I love a good challenge, even if it is uncomfortable. This is why I am growing, evolving and walking the path of my alignment and my authenticity. Not giving up control and not surrendering to The Divine, will keep you stuck. You must release control completely, be prepared to take inspired action, and live in the present moment. Invite Source and your spirit team into your reality and allow them to work on your behalf. They are simply waiting for you to ask. Then get out of your own way and allow things to happen.

Abraham Hicks says, "You find God the moment you realize you don't need to seek God. God is always within us. We are God, God is us."

When we live with a heart of gratitude and show others a gracious hand, when we surrender fully and in faith, true power comes to us. So many of us keep Source's floodgates firmly locked without realizing it. When you believe that you are One with the Universe, and your entire being is of God, how can you possibly question receiving anything good? Source and our angels are waiting for us to clean up our energy, to start learning and allowing instead of complaining or living in judgment and wallowing in negativity.

It's true, of course, that being open to receiving is not always easy. We have likely been taught that it is better to give than to receive, but Source is telling us to open ourselves up to receive fully. And why not? When we open those gates and show a clear and defined faith in Source, our needs and desires will be met.

Here's what I suggest. Try taking on the same attitude you likely had as a child when you went about your days without worry because you knew your needs would be met. This may take some effort at first. As a young adult, life may have handed you a bunch of lessons you weren't ready to receive. Maybe you weren't taught the basic fundamentals of being open to and to look for the lessons—to learn from them and then move on to the next. It's also unlikely you were taught to live in the present moment and to follow your intuition. Perhaps you were taught the fundamentals of religion but not how to properly fuel your soul. If that's the case, I can sympathize.

As I have said before, I had to go through everything I went through to get me where I am and to become who I am today. I am thankful I had that religious base. I am also glad I had experiences of a human and carnal nature. All my experiences—both good, not so good, and challenging—have made me compassionate and understanding as well as full of the flame within. When we realize that flame is always within us, that God is always there, we receive. And remember, we are all One because we are all part of the Eternal Flame. In whatever form Source chooses to show up in our reality, He is always the same fire, and we are all born from that flame.

I'm not sure where I heard this, but I wrote it down, "When we say, 'God is love,' we lose a connection of God and love being energies because we look at love as a feeling or emotion. When we accept love as an energy or vibration, we find the energy of God within us, which is the energy of love."

When we say God is love, we are separating the two. God is the vibration of love. But because we feel the depth of love as warmth in our heart space, we treat it as an emotion. It is not. It is a vibration. When you are in alignment with love, you feel it in your frequency. When you feel your heart swell up and your cup of love overflowing while sitting in prayer or meditation, that is a vibration. When you are petting your dog or cat, and you feel love and peace flowing, that's a vibration we might mistake for an emotion.

When your vibration is love, you will find you will handle life better. There are times when I feel a little off and not immersed in that love, but I can feel my frequency is there just waiting for me to get back into that vibration. The best way to do so is to trust you will.

Below is an example of a letter I wrote to Source to raise my love vibration in order to stay in alignment. Writing love letters expressing my love, trust and truth to Source is something I believe has built and helps maintain a beautiful connection. I wrote this letter when I was at a devastating low point financially and in solitude. Most of my relationships had been pruned from my life, my dad had crossed over, and my love relationship ended. But I was at peace knowing I would be cared for. And I was cared for. Doors opened and continue to open for me because of daily gratitude and unquestioned surrender.

I TRUST YOU, Source.

You know my every desire. You know my heart, mind and soul.

I'm not certain what lies ahead, but I am confident of its unfolding, because you are overseeing all of it.

I know I am worthy to have all of my heart's desires because I am Yours and You are mine. You hold me close to Your Light, and I glow with the energy of Your love.

I trust You. I surrender to You. I give to You my life completely.

I walk in knowing that You have me.

I love you, Source. I love my team of angels, guides and ancestors.

I accept where I am currently because I know it is

teaching me more about who I am in You, and how I am capable of dealing with others. It is showing me that my intuition is spot on, and that the energy of Your love I share makes people feel good about themselves. I am here to show compassion and grace, to give love to all and to be a beacon of Light for You to use and for people to come to. I fully accept my role as student, writer and teacher. Show me where I need to work on myself to become closer to You, Source. My life is Yours, but I also know and realize there are still things that I need to release, and I ask my team of angels to guide me in order to continue healing. I rely on Your love, compassion, mercy and grace. I rely on being fed Your energy to ignite my internal flame, daily. I rely on You to provide for my needs. I trust You have my path laid out and that when You are ready for me to walk down it, You will show me.

I am One with the Universe. I am One with the collective. I am here to be used for Divine purpose. I am here to lead. I know Who I am and in Whom I am and I understand the power I carry. In all of this, it is my purpose to serve humanity and the heavenly realm here on earth.

It is these journal writings, these love letters to God, that have taught me that all Spirit wants is our desire for a connection. Source waits on us to finally give up on our worldly nature and give it all over to be used—the good, bad and ugly of our lives. Because to Source it is all beautiful and can be used in a divine way. Once I surrendered, Source said to me, "I am giving you a blank canvas, paint your desires. This blank canvas is a gift for a job well done—paint your dreams!"

This is where a vision board will come in handy. There is no limit to what you can dream about or put on that board. Mine has "New York Times Best Seller" and a microphone with me on stage teaching, doing a TedTalk, and a mock picture of the book I am writing with my angelic team. It has travel destinations all over the world, eating healthy and hitting the gym with my divine partner. It also has my dream house and car. There are also things on it that are of the spiritual nature, like angels and meditation.

My oldest daughter did this last year as well. She put on hers that she wanted to pay off my parents house and buy my mom a car, and she actually did that this year. Thankfully, because my dad passed away and her doing so left my mom without the stress of a house payment.

Source knew what was coming and Source also knew that was a desire of my daughter's heart and so made it happen for all of them. I know people put some crazy dreams on their boards, and when they come to fruition, the crazy dream becomes a reality. Source is also asking us to dream bigger! Flow the big energy from your soul and believe you can attain that crazy dream. This allows Source to make big things happen in your life. Looking at a dream board every single day instills your heart's desires in you. It takes a lot of strength to dream big and believe it can happen, you just need faith and an unwavering belief in what you and Source will achieve together.

I have stepped into the strength that has always been within me. Before, I was just too full of everything Source is not, to be able to find it. But as the outer shell of who I thought I was began to fade away, my inner beauty appeared. You have to dig for diamonds. They aren't on the surface of the earth. They are valuable because of the long process of creation and growth they have to go through under the earth. It takes immense pressure and extreme temperatures for a diamond to form. It takes between one billion and 3.3 billion years! It also requires a great amount of time and effort to dig deep and uncover them.

What those times of pressure and extremes have given me is an understanding of my true nature and how to regulate my emotions. I think finally figuring out how to have control over my emotions, using them and not allowing them to use me, is what has changed my reality most. Release the past version of yourself, but most importantly, release any negative thoughts you are holding about someone else. Just as you have had the opportunity to change and continue to evolve, trust that Source is also working on everyone else in your life. We all have the opportunity to become a new and awakened being. Believe in the change, not only in yourself, but that the collective of humanity and the world can shift and change for the better. If you harbor ill will against another, or if you continue to judge, you cannot and will not evolve. In a sense you are energetically trying to hold another back. Let go and surrender, learn to love and live continually with the God vibration. And to be honest, there are people I just don't like. I love everyone, but there's a few I'm not crazy about, they ain't my cup of tea. Trust me, it's okay to have those feelings. I just don't give those few people a second thought and realize that the feelings or emotions I do have for certain people are for my protection. Remember this, what you damn, will most certainly damn you back. So be careful of the words and judgments you may be tempted to express, especially those you have against God. We have free will, which means we are free to speak against our circumstances, other people or the Universe, but it's important to keep in mind that speaking against them will bring negative energy into our life.

LIfe is a process that unfolds in stages—the earthly stages of birth, adolescence, teen years, marriage, family, aging and death. We go through many more spiritual stages than we do human stages, but we likely do not realize they are happening. I think one of the best ways to explain this is through the life stages of a butterfly. Often during a lifetime we are a caterpillar, then a chrysalis, and then we emerge as a butterfly. For every new job, sport, hobby or evolution we choose to start anew, we become a caterpillar all over again to eventually go through the stages and become a butterfly once again.

Butterflies don't live a long time, and the same goes for situations in certain times of our lives. We are constantly evolving. Old ways and ideas are dying, and there's a need to let go. That is why we should always follow our dreams and not people. Some people know they have intuition and yet they neglect to check in with it, but most people are so lost, they don't even know they have intuition. This is why following your own path is the wisest one to take.

Here's something else it's important to know. There's a reason observing the sabbath is one of the Ten Commandments. It doesn' have to be on a particular day, but every so often we need to slow down, take a break, and recharge, just as God rested on the seventh day after six days of creation.

Source wants us to know and to understand that we can't give energy we don't have. You know that saying, "You can't fill from an empty cup." Well, a vision I once received was an electric plug in power strip. You plug the power strip in the wall outlet and that will power perhaps ten plugs.

Think of yourself as the power strip and Source as the power source. Everyone is plugging into you to get your beautiful, clean energy, and you, in turn, become energetically depleted from it. There comes a time that you must unplug everyone and everything from you and plug yourself into Source to recharge. That is how you continue to get energy for all of those "butterfly" stages you continually go through.

Source also wants us to know that when we show gratitude for the little things as much as we do the big things and surrender to the will of the Universe, we can and will be unstoppable. Can you imagine if everyone were able to find the path they're intended to be on, how incredible an instrument of change we could be—all of us working together? When we live in love, we not only continue to build bridges connecting all of us, we become a Light and a flame for Source. When the flame inside us is willing to surrender the "who" we think we are in this human form, to the Who that is inside of us watching, we will live life in a constant flow state.

We also need to embrace the idea that two or more flames can glow at the same time. No one has to put a flame out in someone else in order to become brighter. When we glow together, the flames put off more light.

Surrender with gratitude, allow changes to unfold, stand before Source and allow your life to be used for divine purpose. Allow the flame within you to burn with a deep love and watch your life change, living in your purpose.

Chapter Eight

Fill Me with the Flame

I had all of the chapters laid out in order a couple of months ago soon after I'd started this book, and this chapter was supposed to be, "Dedication to the Path." But when taking my bath today, Source let me know what the title and subject of this chapter needed to be. In my spiritual walk, and in most religions, numbers are significant. In the Bible, threes and sevens are prominent. In my spiritual life, eight is the number of Infinity. Source is the Universe and the Universe is Infinite. So this is Chapter Eight, my personal synonym for Infinity, and Source let me know the subject of it should be, "Fill Me with the Flame."

Let me backup a few days and tell you the backstory about this. All day long I was seeing double and triple numbers on license plates, road signs, on the clock and on receipts. I'm aware this is how my angels and guides communicate with me, so I pay attention to numbers, words, names and colors I repeatedly see or hear. This particular day I was seeing double and triple eights and twos everywhere. I always thank them for giving me these signs, and because of this, I am blessed with constant communication from them. I was heading to someone's house to drop off something, and I was going through a ritual as I drove, talking to my angels to thank them for the day, and for always making sure my needs are met. Then I came to a stop light, I was the fourth car back on the inside lane, and I saw 144 on a license plate in front of me, and the car next to it had 333 on it, another car had 4488, and the one next to it, 888. I laughed and joked with my angels about how they made that happen.

I said, "I love you guys! I love all of the signs you show me!"

Then I went a few blocks and a car cut me off. Before I could say or feel anything, I looked at the plate and it read three letters plus 2288. Because I am completely into this and say stupid stuff, I said, "two, two, eight, eight. Eighty eight, two eights... Deuce deuce eight eight! Hey! That's not only infinity, that's double infinity!"

I know, don't judge. I got back home, opened my computer and one of my favorite tarot readers had just put out a new Virgo video on YouTube. I only have a few readers I follow because I know I get accurate messages sent through them. They are conduits for Divine messages to me. No, tarot is not evil. Much like everything else, even the Bible, it can be used for evil, but in this case it is not.

I started the Virgo reading on Searchlight Tarot and she pulled out the Hermit card, which is the Virgo card, and on it was a book. The next card was a solitude oracle card that had a girl reading the Book of Knowledge. Of course, this meant something to me since I was writing a book.

Then she pointed out two 8's in the spread and said, "INFINITY!" I was geeking out at this point, and after the reading I got in a hot epsom salts bath. I began talking to Source and angels and went into meditation.

While meditating, I could feel my third eye open. When this happens, I can see the cosmos and the stars in the depths of space. Then it went into a very clear picture and the picture was me sitting on my couch typing on my

MacBook. I appeared to be in a trance-like state, with the glow of the computer screen on my face. I was typing very fast, and my head was going left to right. When I zoomed in on my fingers, I could see they were glowing, moving fast over the keys, and I realized I was unaware of what was happening. The angels were using my fingers to type.

I was still in the bath, deep into this meditation, one hand hanging outside the tub, when my cat bit my finger—it scared the you-know-what out of me! I guess the angels didn't want me to see too much and used my cat to stop me before I got too far into the vision.

When I meditate, I am given words that I whisper, and I was given, "Fill me with the flame." I instantly knew that this was meant to be the eighth chapter of this book.

Let me say, I am not prepared to write this chapter. The key points, yes, but I must rely on the rest to be given to me as I go, to which I must say, "What else is new?" That's how my journey has been, so I'm well equipped to do things, as we say in the restaurant world, "On the fly." Honestly, I haven't had to research or prepare much while writing this book. It has been fed to me, and what has come through the most is what I was guided to journal. It's kind of crazy how all that fell into place for me, as well. Anyway, let's get on with being filled with the Flame of the Holy Spirit and lighting the torch within.

I had a dreamlike vision when I knew I was moving past the healing phase of my journey. In this vision, I was walking through a dark tunnel. I wasn't sure if it was underground, or if it was built inside a mountain, but the walls were definitely dirt and looked as though they were smooth, but ruddy, as though they'd been scooped out with a shovel. I was wearing clothes that appeared to be from biblical times—layers of cloth with large sleeves. The bottom of it was dirty because it was dragging on the ground. I was holding a small, lit torch as I made my way. The tunnel was like a labyrinth. It had many different ways one could go.

I was moving slowly, being cautious, because I was uncertain what might lie ahead. I remember feeling uneasy in my dream, and so I was trying to breathe quietly. I would pause between steps and listen in an effort to hear if anyone or anything was nearby.

I felt exhausted, sat down on the ground and fell asleep. When I woke up, standing in front of me was an old, yet youthful looking man. He was dressed all in white cloth—the same type of material I was wearing—but his robe was pristine, almost glowing white, and he had a long beard that was also radiant. He had on a little red hat that fit snugly on his head, the bluest eyes, and he was carrying a massive torch with a flame that was yellow, orange and blue. I looked up at him and did not feel any fear at all.

He smiled at me and said to stand and follow him, which I did. I had faith this man had my back—I trusted him. He never said a word to me, but he looked back at me every so often and gave me a slight grin.

We arrived at a pool of water, which I now suspected was inside a cavern. The water was turquoise blue, and it seemed to glow. It was so beautiful that it took my breath away. The man in white told me to cup my hands and take a drink, and so I did.

The water was ice cold, but as it went down, it felt like a soothing warm tea coating my throat. I stood up, and he approached me, torch in hand, and looked me in the eye. I looked deeply into his clear blue eyes and could see the light of the torch dancing in them.

He said, "You have the Flame within, and you have had a drink of the water of life. It is your time to share your internal fire with those who are seeking."

That's when I woke up and understood that it was an angel that found me while I was looking for the path I needed to walk. This angel led me to the water of life, and the flame I saw in his eyes was also in mine. This vision showed me that I was ready to begin on my path and that it was time to be who my soul wanted me to be in this incarnation.

I don't remember most of my dreams, but I certainly remembered this one. It was as though I was actually there, and perhaps I was—or I should say that my soul was actually there. After this vision, I had a deep understanding of the Flame and how it is lit when we are ready to give up our old ways and follow the direction Source would have us go. I completely shifted after that vision and have not felt inadequate since. I knew it was telling me of the power I have within and without. I now know with every fiber of who I am that I am protected and have the power of the Holy Spirit backing me in order to live my calling. The dream showed me who I truly am and the angel looking me in the eye taught me that I am worthy of abundant love.

I've had dreams since then that have given me guidance, but this one changed who I am. Source gives us a great deal of guidance through dreams and visions, but in our busy day to day lives we often choose to ignore them. Some are scary and will shake us up. I have to say, dreams like that are most likely from Source and are intended to create change within you. When you're filled with the Flame you experience the pure essence of Source, you are so on fire internally, you can't imagine a day of not feeling the deep connection.

Throughout religious texts and teachings, the words fire or flame are used to describe the Source within us, as well as to indicate purification and communing with The Divine. In Christianity, fire is used to describe the Holy Spirit, which indicates renewal, divine presence and purification. As you probably know, tongues of fire descended upon the disciples during Pentecost. Moses saw and spoke God in the form of a burning bush, and when we are being purified, it is said that we are refined by the fire (see Zechariah 13:9). Leviticus 9:24 says, "God Himself lit the fire. And because of this, it became holy fire, and though the Hand of God touched it, it was never to be allowed to go out."

Native American religions use fire in various rituals to connect with the spirit world when they dance in the illumination of the sun. They use fire in sweat lodge ceremonies or pipe ceremonies as a means of purification and healing.

Buddhists regard fire or flame as a symbol of purification or transformation. It is also how they refer to, "the self." For them fire symbolizes whatever it is we mistake for self that we believe is lasting and unaffected by the world. They also use the terms "inner-fire" or "inner-light" to refer to spiritual awakening, or the nature of enlightenment. They use fire to burn offerings and to purify negative energies.

In Africa, fire is a symbol for purification, transformation and communicating with ancestors. They use it to cleanse spiritual spaces and to communicate with the spirit world. It is also associated with vitality and life force.

The eternal flame in Judaism is lit and kept burning in holy temples. The flame represents the divine presence of God and serves as a reminder of the miracle of the burning bush.

In Hinduism, fire is considered sacred and also symbolizes purification when used for the heart and mind in rituals. It is always used to invoke blessings and to communicate with the Hindu god of fire, Agni. It's also used in rite of passage ceremonies for birth, marriage and death. Hindus believe—and I love this—that "fire is the only element that cannot be polluted."

In Islam, fire is mentioned as punishment in the afterlife for those who are disobedient to Allah. It is also used in purification rituals.

The Emerald Tablets of Thoth refer to the "Life Flame" or "the flame" numerous times in the 15 tablets. T3 V45 reads, "Pour forth thy flame as a Sun of the morning. Shut out the darkness and live in the day." T4 V13; reads, ".... Lift up your flame from out of the darkness, fly from the night and ye shall be free."

There are so many verses that refer to the flame. In spirituality, The Golden Flame of Illumination is the spark that awakens consciousness. This is when you discover your true and authentic nature, when you awaken to and have knowledge of Self and experience an expansion of consciousness. The flame is where the Light of God exists, and so there can exist no darkness within me.

A flame is also used to represent two minds coming together with the intention of creating a single, powerful consciousness.

During the past two years, I have increasingly felt as though Source was guiding me to write about the fire or flame within, and I wrote about it in a number of journal entries. I'm being guided to share what I journaled in the hope that it might open your heart and soul in order to allow a flame to be lit in you.

One of my most powerful recurring experiences is when my heart feels as though it is being warmed by a flame. Most of the time, it happens during meditation. I don't want to delve too deeply into my meditation practices now, but I will do so in an upcoming chapter. In this one, I will write about my experiences of being refined and purified by the fire during the last several years. In that regard, one of the most basic, yet prolific times on my journey was when I could feel the burning away of the old within me. What Source wants and requires from us is to be sanctified and to live in truth. This truth is to live with a pure conscience, free of untruths and judgments.

During the times I was going through "lessons," as well as in times of deep transformation, I finally realized what being "refined by the fire" meant, both figuratively as well as within my body. I could feel the old being burned away, and as the old was leaving, I began to feel the eternal flame within me.

I now feel the flame in every energy center.

I've mentioned the feeling in my chest a few times—the feeling of a warming, comforting love. It remains within constantly like warm, glowing embers, but when I feel the love of Source, or gratitude, compassion, or any other form of high vibration love, those embers burst into flame.

This brings to mind a metaphor. When metal is refined, oxygen is added to the impure liquid metal and the impurities oxidize before the metal is removed. It seems to me we are refined in much the same way. Source is the oxygen that is added to impure human beings to separate us from our impurities. In other words, when Source blows on the embers within us, they become like a fire burning within.

Once the process is complete, and it can take numerous times depending on the impurities we need to release, we become refined. That's when we begin to live our lives in a manner that is no longer pleasing to our flesh, but is pleasing to Source, and I can assure you that once you go through this process, pleasing Source is the absolute most important aspect of your life.

Back when I was going to church, the term, "refined by the fire," was thrown around like it was an everyday occurrence. Because I was a Christian, I presumably was on the path to being refined. The belief was that all I needed to do was to let go of a few things. Later, I learned about the true process, which involves the alchemy of our total existence, physical and spiritual, and I embraced it. I must tell you it is not a process for the weak. Those who go through it are forced to look deep within every part of their being and see clearly things they never want to see again. I'm referring to the lies that were told, the dishonest things that were done. What a person thought was hidden comes back to them in full color. Nothing is untouched.

I spent three years going through the process. It started slowly, and at first what was given to me to burn up was the easy stuff. But, as I went along, the hard things began to surface. I would alchemize them as quickly as possible and ask for more so that I could get through it. Just when I thought I was done, however, the heavenly realms said, "Not so fast. There's an unhealed something that's still within you. You need to let go of it and throw it into the fire in order to burn it away."

It's hard to go through it, but it's also beautiful when you look back after it's done and you know you did the work. You know you have released it from yourself and from the generations that will follow. It happens because Source loves us. Source wants us to evolve, to awaken spiritually, and the act of being refined by the divine flame shows how much love there is for us. Once you come out of the fire, your thoughts and motives change. It is no longer about trying to impress others, it is about being someone in the eyes of the spirit realm. It is about knowing you need to live in a way that respects not only yourself and others, but the Divinity who loves you and chose you to be one who lives with purpose.

The Bible says that the Holy Spirit refines followers by the conviction of "sins," which we then need to confess and repent. What is often missed is the actual refinement within us. We can talk a big game, say we have done the work and that we have confessed our wrong doings and will do them no more. But the refining part may never truly happen. It's not enough just to say the words. One must do the internal work of letting it all go. One must work through it on an intimate level with Source.

So be honest and clear with yourself. How intimate are you with Source? How much time do you actually spend in the presence of Source where you aren't thinking about other things you need to do, or all of the stuff that you need to ask for? If you do not have a relationship with Source that leaves you standing internally and spiritually naked and fully exposed, you are living a lie with respect to your true relationship.

I believe, there really isn't "sin." I think we use that word to describe the ugly side of human nature. What we consider to be sin is actually who we are with respect to our polarity. Everyone has a shadow side. We all have Dr. Jekyll and Mr. Hyde within us. What we consider to be "sin" are actually those things we do to pinch ourselves off from Source energy. It's a word that was used by those who created religion to promulgate disparaging feelings towards doing or being what society deemed as unacceptable or wrong. Of course we are all "sinners." We could just as correctly say, "We are all human," and leave religion out of it.

The word "sin" has created so much dissension within the human race that it has taken on a more powerful meaning for those who are not awakened than the truly powerful words, "love, compassion and forgiveness." The amount of hate that has come from the word "sin" is huge. To make them feel better about themselves, many people take on a self-righteous persona and stand in judgment of those who live differently than they do. They're the ones who throw out the word, "sinner!"

It's impossible for anyone to be perfect. Those who throw stones at others are usually the ones who live in glass houses, figuratively speaking. As Jesus said in Luke 6:41, "Why do you notice the splinter in your brother's eye, but do not perceive the wooden beam in your own?"

Until you refine your "sins" completely, they are always there. Remember, what is done in the dark will always come out into the light, especially when you are so adamant about how perfectly you live your life and how imperfectly someone else is living theirs.

With all of that said, until you can set your human nature aside, you will live in a constant cycle of chasing your tail, and you will struggle to live your truth and pursue your true calling. You'll always be asking yourself why the same things come around and happen to you again and again. It is because you have not allowed your human nature to be burned away. You haven't stood naked before Source and had all of you exposed. It is because you have chosen to continue to rely solely upon yourself.

I stand back and watch people continue on their spiral of life. I want to tell them that with a few years of work they could come to terms with the truth of who they are, and then be free and able to live here on earth in the sanctuary of Source and the heavenly realms.

I can't imagine going back to my old life. You could hand me a million dollars to go back to my old ways, and I would walk away and continue on the path with Source. There's nothing that feels better than being connected. It may seem hard at first. Source heals us slowly, and so it doesn't happen overnight. It almost always takes time. But doing the work and allowing the work to be done within you will set you free. Based on my experience, finally living life on your own terms and with divine guidance is the way, perhaps the only way, to live a full life.

Once filled with the flame, you will have the deep desire to show love to all people, all animals and to our earth. After learning about all of the different religions and faiths, I now see how much they are alike. Not only is the Golden Rule practically universal, each faith also agrees about the power of purification by fire and the cleansing nature of water. So, beyond the superficial differences, all are virtually the same. It follows that the way to a peaceful world, what Jesus called the Kingdom of Heaven on Earth, is to create a bridge on which to carry buckets of love to one another.

There truly is only one religion in all of the world, which is the worship of God, Source, The Divine, The Universe, Allah, Yahweh, Creator, or Father. Whatever we choose to call it, the bond of love is the bond of each faith. Everything in addition to that is something humans have conjured up, taught, preached, and passed to future generations as being the truth.

Our truth is knowing that Source is love, and that we, too, are love. The world around us will thrive when we pour out that love on each other.

We are all flame born. We have the fire within us that is Source. We are created in the image of a beautiful fire that will light up the dark. Because we have that same fire inside, we can also light up rooms and the people around us. In whatever form Source decides to show up, our hearts and bodies are prepared to accept Him with love and mercy. We're open to being used in infinite ways. As I have said before, we are sparks from the flame of love and the flame is God. All are one because we are all part of the same eternal flame.

Our consciousness evolves as we move through the levels of awakening. We transform during a time of purging and the transmutation of energies. Eventually, we graduate and are initiated into a new level of being, a new level of elevated consciousness.

A spiritual initiate is one who has achieved an initial shift in consciousness to a higher plateau, and is now on his or her way to ever higher levels. Typically, humans start out with carnal or animalistic outlooks on life. To ignite the flame within requires an increase in vibration, an elevated frequency, which happens through the process of self examination. Dr. Carl Jung, who was born in 1875 and died in 1961, is known among other things for the concept of individuation. He said, "Until you make the unconscious conscious, it will direct your life and call it fate."

If you do not seek to ignite the flame by going within, you will not step onto the path to enlightenment, but do not despair. Enlightenment may not be your soul's primary goal this time around. One thing is certain, however. Your soul's goal for each and every incarnation is to grow and evolve by meeting and overcoming the challenges you face on earth. Life in a physical body is difficult by design because overcoming challenges builds character, perseverance, and wisdom. But whatever your primary reason for being here this time may be, your soul also desires to participate in the spirit realm while here, and this is absolutely the case if you are one of The Chosen.

No matter who you are, or why you are here, your mission is not to accumulate material wealth or tangible goods—as our western culture would have us believe. Money and material riches cannot buy happiness or fulfillment. What will bring peace and fulfillment, perhaps even joy, is using your skills and abilities to serve others in a meaningful way. For The Chosen that means bringing the intangible, spiritual element into this world and serving others with love.

Let's face it. When our bodies die, we do not and we cannot take anything tangible with us. However, whatever good you do while here, you are depositing into a heavenly bank account to enjoy later—after you cross over. As Jesus told the rich young ruler in Mark 17:21, "Go, sell everything you have and give to the poor, and you will have treasure in heaven." And Matthew 6:19-21 says, "Do not lay up for yourselves treasures on earth, where moth and rust destroy and where thieves break in and steal, but lay up for yourselves treasures in heaven, where neither moth nor rust destroys and where thieves do not break in and steal. For where your treasure is, there your heart will be also." In other words, the money and material possessions you accumulate in this lifetime will remain here on Earth when you die, but the good you do for others will pile up mind blowing riches that you can and will enjoy in the afterlife. You might just decide to change the direction of your life if you give that some thought and take it to heart.

When you do decide to value your spirit side and take action in that regard, you will also begin to create your own heaven here on earth. Our spirit naturally wants to be rid of anything on our path that will keep us from being compatible with this new reality. In this life, all I can say is, "Be as happy as the Buddha, loving as Jesus and follow your own compass." Your internal compass will guide you on what is called, "Your true north."

Our life path is guided by our North Node. If you understand what your North Node in your natal chart is, you will understand your calling. (If you don't have a birth chart, you can get one free from Astrology.com.) When you light your internal flame and go through the stages of spiritual transformation, you will know what the best path for you is during this incarnation.

Being refined by the fire is worth it. Once we get through the initial levels successfully and are able to balance our energies, we will quickly recover if we do get knocked off balance. We will not lay up treasures on earth, where moth and rust destroy and where thieves break in and steal because we will no longer allow the world around us to determine the way we respond. We will rely solely on the direction of Source and know our team of angels and guides will take care of any business that needs to be tended to on our behalf. Our job will be to stay awake and open to what we are being guided to do and then show up and do the job.

Alice A. Bailey, a channeler who lived in the 1920's, wrote about Theosophy and the concept of Initiation. She said there are nine levels of spiritual development, and there are four basic levels that humans can progress through with each incarnation. Once souls have advanced to the fourth level of initiation, they have achieved enlightenment; and have no further need to reincarnate. On the fifth level and beyond, souls have the opportunity to become members of the Spiritual Hierarchy.

The only way to attain this is to raise your level of consciousness. This begins with the dedication of meditative practices and finding that fire that burns within your soul. More will be written about this in the upcoming chapter.

Chapter Nine

Meditation, the Pathway to Love

One morning while driving to work, I was talking to Source and my spirit team about how my life was going and how grateful I am for every earthly thing I have. I'm thankful for my children, grandchildren, my family and most of all my good health. I thanked them for my ability to work and to provide for myself, but I said, "At some point, I dream of having a beautiful love story."

I'd never experienced that. Oh, I thought I'd been in love, but now I realize I wasn't. I'd attracted partners that could not be trusted who harbored negative emotions or feelings from unreleased past trauma. As previously mentioned, like attracts like, and so whatever your vibrational level happens to be is exactly what you're going to attract.

After I made that statement about desiring a beautiful love story, Source responded to me so clearly, "Oh, my Love, what you are living in Me, is a true love story".

I smiled because I felt the absolute truth of that. Once we do the work on ourselves and allow Source energy to guide our paths, the love and compassion for others begins to flow from us. I know that when I was going through the transformative part of this journey, I was trying to find the ability deep within me to love certain strangers and some of my acquaintances. It was so difficult, but I knew an obstacle within was holding me back and that I needed to allow whatever it was to heal. This is an issue for a lot of us because we are conditional when it comes to how we deal with others. I knew I needed to find that love, but it was hard. Frankly, it took time and a lot of meditation to help me get to that point.

I think meditation was the catalyst that helped me overcome the challenge. It was through my meditation practices that helped catapult me to my awakening and ultimately changed every aspect of my life. The one aspect I love more than anything is the connection and the ability to hear the voice of Source and the angels around me, which happens through meditation. I have also so enjoyed the unfolding of this journey I'm on and discovering who I truly am.

The Archangels want me to focus on meditation in this chapter because without doubt, it is the practice I used daily to heal and transform myself, and it is what I now use every day to stay in alignment.

If you'd asked me years ago if I meditate, I'd have laughed and said, "Heck no!" If you were to ask me now, I would say, hands down, it is the key we need to meet ourselves as well as Source, and to come together to share our love with all of humanity. I absolutely believe it is the first step to take in order to form a bridge of love that connects all people.

It wasn't easy for me when I began to practice meditation. My ego mind was running the show back then. As soon as I began, my nose would itch, and then I'd try to find a comfortable position, but I couldn't decide where to put my arms and hands. I would think incessantly about everything under the sun. Then I'd get frustrated and give up.

Let me tell you a few things I have learned along the way that helped me. YouTube has many guided meditations from which to choose. Start with a ten minute video first thing in the morning. Get up a few minutes earlier than usual and connect with Source to start your day. Do the meditation before your morning cup of coffee because caffeine will make your ability to remain calm more difficult.

Some YouTube meditations will teach you how to breathe, which is a key to being able to go deep into it. Since "practice makes perfect," you'll get better at this as time goes by.

One thing I learned that was a big obstacle for me is that it's okay to have a thought. Just recognize that your mind drifted for a moment. Do not judge the thought—allow it to pass. You'll be amazed at how quickly you connect. For instance, I might be thinking about my breathing. Then, suddenly, thoughts about some random thing will come to mind. I realize it's there but do not let myself become attached to it. Instead, I allow it to play out without analyzing or judging it. Then I return to my breathing and visualization.

If I am doing chakra or energy centers work, I concentrate on each center without judgment or any attempt to force something to happen. The different chakra colors will come up in my mind's eye, which is an indication I have unblocked the chakra and it's time to move to the next.

Early on, I would become frustrated because I was trying to focus on the orange glow for the sacral chakra, but the yellow solar plexus glow kept popping up instead. Now I just allow whatever needs to happen to happen. I now realize the chakra may have something to say to me—maybe it wants my attention. It took me about a year to become fairly good at this, and I still can't say that I have risen to the Buddhist Monk level by any means.

If you can sit or lie down facing the east or north east, that is the best. This is the direction from which earth's magnetic energy is generated. According to Hindu teaching, the northeast corner is known as Ishan, "The Corner for God." I have had the most intense meditation experiences when facing that direction.

After a while of doing guided meditations in order to learn the techniques that work best for you, you'll be able to meditate on your own without them. I look forward to this tranquil time with my Higher Self and Source. If you are at all like me, you'll crave the energy and peace you get from them.

I find it's much like going to the gym. You really don't want to go until you get there. But when you've finished, you're happy you did it. Trust me, the time you take to get centered is time well spent. It makes those obstacles that pop up in life easier to face because you become filled up with energies not found in the 3-D world. You've been recharged with the love energy of Source.

I want to share with you the story of a particular meditation that changed me, exponentially. When it happened, I'd been meditating sporadically for about five years. I feel it was a "Kundalini Awakening," because everything shifted for me, after which I began to feel a constant connection with Source. My frequency has remained elevated since then.

It happened on the night of a new moon in Virgo, which is my astrological sun, rising, and my Venus sign. This was two weeks after my birthday, during which there was a full super moon and a blue moon. It was also two weeks after my dad's passing and four days after I'd ended the long term relationship I told you about.

I wrote in my journal as I usually do, but on the night of a new moon, I also do a "new moon ceremony," which is when I write down what I am releasing. I ask Source to show me what I need to work on, or through, in order to stay in alignment. (Side note: Moon phases are times for releasing or transmutation and for manifesting your dreams.) If needed, I'll also do cord-cutting ceremonies, or whatever else I might be guided to do by my angels. On those nights, I always take an epsom salts bath, and I wash my crystals and energy stones and set them out for energy cleansing.

That particular night, I finished journaling, wrote down what I was releasing, and did a cord cutting as well as all of my usual traditions. I then went outside and stood on a little patch of grass and did some grounding. I closed my eyes and felt the energy around and within me.

I came back into my apartment and sat on my couch, which was facing east, and closed my eyes. I began to meditate to clear my chakras and quickly saw all the colors unfold from the red root chakra to my violet crown chakra.

This night's meditation was different from usual. Out loud, I started saying what I was releasing. I began to cry, but not tears of sadness or pain. They were tears of love and of feeling deeply connected.

I sat quietly and Source began to give me single words to say. I would softly say them out loud—a lot of positive and good feeling words all strung together: "Love, compassion, grounding, heart, peace, joy—"

Then I started to breathe differently than normal. I sucked in cold air quickly through my mouth, then exhaled slowly but somewhat forcefully. I did this about ten times, and then started breathing intensely through my nose—feeling the cold air in my head space. Then I slowly released the breath.

I was fed words again, and I repeated them. They were words of love and gratitude. My heart space was warm. I could feel Source blowing on those embers, and the fire within became fully stoked.

Sitting there, I felt as though I was outside of my body, floating. Then I felt my root chakra heat up. I could feel the heat go up through my spine—then the sensation of my crown chakra opening. I literally felt as though I was floating.

My body seemed to expand. My hands felt as though they were getting bigger and then it was my entire body growing larger.

Next, I felt a bubble around me that seemed to be gold in color, which made me feel completely protected and at ease.

I remained in that trance for quite some time—I didn't want it to stop.

Finally, my third eye began to open. I saw the cosmos and the stars, and then I was shown my life's path and the journey I was about to embark upon. That is why I am writing this book with so much confidence in my future, because the future was shown to me at that point, and it has been shown to me many times since.

When I was released from this meditation, which lasted about an hour or so, I felt incredibly clean. I know that is strange to say, but I felt as if I was super clean and so full of peace, joy and love. The bubble has been around me since then. It is my bubble of protection—it protects my precious energies.

Nothing earthly can compare to the love frequency I took from that medication, or from any of my quiet times with Source.

Sometimes when I meditate, I simply have a conversation with the Archangels. You can also call it prayer, I suppose, but it's less formal. I ask and they answer. They also ask me questions that cause me to think and to go within. During such times, I often spend time laughing because they are rather funny. Meditation connects me directly to the etheric realm. Our angels and spirit guides want us to connect with them, and it's possible to do so through this practice.

Let me tell you another meditation story. Like the one above, it was extremely life-changing for me. It happened on a day I was off of work, so I cooked for a client and spent most of my day writing and meditating. During meditation that morning, while I was connected to Source, I asked what I'd done in my prior life. Often, I have to wait for an answer, and I know I need to be on the alert for signs and synchronicities because the answer will always come.

I asked this because I have always felt as though I was destined to write and to teach, and deep within it didn't seem that writing and teaching was new to me. I have always loved spelling and learning new words. Anyone who knows me well will tell you that I find power in words—how words are used is important to me. I was also having visions of the place where I'd lived in that past life, but I'd been unable to connect it with anything I'd seen in pictures.

That evening, I had to make a delivery to one of my clients. I remained in my car, and waited outside of his gym for him to pick it up. Having arrived a little early, I opened my car's sunroof, closed my eyes, and immediately began seeing white flashes. Then, all of the sudden, the North Node symbol appeared—really white and really bright.

At that time, I knew what most of my birth chart placements were, but not my North Node. I had to look up what the upside down horseshoe symbol represented. I'd seen it before but wasn't exactly sure what it meant. When I get these types of signs, my angels want me to do some research, and so when I got home, I read what I could find about the North and South Nodes.

I learned that my North Node is in Aquarius, and the South Node is the sign opposite it on the Zodiac, which is Leo. I began watching videos on YouTube and was surprised by what I learned. I realized I was at the beginning of the search I needed to undertake to answer the question I'd asked that morning. Placements in the North Node dictate present life energy and your direction or path in this life. Placements of the South Node depict past life energy and your past life experiences.

I was all in to explore this rabbit hole and so began to research Aquarius North Node and Leo South Node. I found that my North Node says that I tend to approach life with a sense of compassion, charisma, and individuality. My South Node says that I feel comfortable in the spotlight. All of this is very true of my basic personality. I began to ask, "What does this mean? How does this answer the question?"

After researching what I could find on the subject, I began to meditate. Then Archangel Michael started to communicate with me. I was told to get my divination rods and the individual alphabet letters I have written on post-it notes.

If you haven't heard of divination rods, they are copper dowsing rods that were used to find water underground years ago when someone needed to dig a well. Someone adept at this would hold the rods and walk around until they came over a water source, which would cause the rods to vibrate.

These rods also work in another way. When you hold these copper rods in each hand, the energy of the spirit you're communicating with moves them from side to side. So I set the letter post-it notes on the counter, and Archangel Michael would move the rods to the letter he wanted me to write down.

He gave me the letters W-E-I-L, and then an S.

I said, "What does this mean?"

I was then told to look up the name Weil and that the first name started with an S. So, I Googled that, and much to my surprise, someone named Simone Weil came up. I'd never heard of her. I sat there and just stared at the image, thinking to myself that like me, she had curly hair and wore glasses. I will tell you, it wasn't long before my heart sank down into my stomach, and I cried. My human, ego self had no idea, but my soul knew. I was connected to this human and the connection is that we are the same soul but we now occupy and have occupied different physical bodies.

As I researched, I realized the essence of who she was and who I am are parallel in many ways. She was born in 1909 and crossed back over to the other side in 1943 at the age of 34. She was a French teacher, philosopher, mystic and political activist. I was once very involved in politics, but I left that behind in order to fully experience the peace and joy I now have.

She received a Bachelors and a Masters Degree at the University of Paris. I'd often wondered why I was chosen to write a book even though I don't have a college education. Now I understand why I was told I was prepared. On a soul level I'm college educated, and that has come with me into this life. In addition, what I am doing is on a divine level.

She became a teacher and political activist who fought for the working class. She was religious and inclined towards mysticism. She was also a writer but was not published until the 1950's and 1960's—years after her death. She'd read numerous religious texts, and also had the desire to understand the beliefs and teachings of different religious traditions. All my life I've been interested in different faiths—I've found them fascinating. It's definitely a core value I carry within my soul. Simone is evidence of that to me. I could go on and on about her life, but try to keep it short. My life has been pretty boring compared to hers, but our desires were and are very much the same.

Frankly, learning about who I was in my most recent past life put me in a state of awe. Before finding out about Simone, I joked with my daughters that I hoped I would be published while I'm still alive. Now I understand where that desire came from.

I am carrying on the legacy of sweet Simone and her heart full of compassion and fight. Her published writings are based on the love of God. Some of them emphasize how affliction and pain are what often drive people toward God. Among other divinely guided writings, she journaled, and some of those journals have been turned into books. I would encourage you to read them. One of her most famous quotes is, "Attention is the rarest form of generosity. It is given to very few minds to notice that things and beings exist. Since my childhood I have not wanted anything else but to receive the complete revelation of this before dying."

I would agree. People are often so consumed with their own stories that they forget that others have stories to share as well. It's important to share the precious time we have—to take time to be generous with it and to focus attention on someone who has something they want to say. It can mean a great deal to them.

Returning to my North and South nodes, who I am in this life and who I was in the past one are pretty much in line astrologically. Simone was an Aquarius sun sign, as am I, which seems to be synchronistic. I feel that's a form of confirmation from the Universe. Imagine. I was able to realize all this and make the connection because of a brief time of meditation, and because I was open to the Universe's promptings. Of course, another important part was following through and taking action.

I originally wasn't going to share what's coming next, but I am being prompted to do so by my angels. This is a story of a past life regression hypnosis session I was a part of, so let me give you the backstory first. I say this because it is amazing how the things I ask for fall into place.

Before what I will describe took place, I was having dreams of being in Egypt in ancient times. I woke up one particular morning and asked my angels why I kept having those dreams. I also told them I was ready to meet people in my soul tribe. Most people in my current life had been removed from it, and I was a couple months out of solitude. I was ready to meet new friends in this dimension, and intuitively I knew they would soon be coming into my life.

When I know I am going to write for the day, and this was one of those days, I take a hot epsom salts bath to cleanse my body. I drink plenty of water, and I cleanse my space by walking through my apartment with a burning sage bundle, and that day I needed to go to the "woo woo" store to get a new sage bundle. The one I had was burned down to a nub.

Going to the "woo woo" store is always fun for me. The owner and I talk about metaphysical happenings and flow energy through one another. It's a place where I can be open and no one looks at me as if I'm crazy.

As we were talking, I was telling her how I was shown that I was Simone Weil in my previous life.

She said, "You should sign up to do the past life regression hypnosis tomorrow night."

I'm sure it was not a coincidence that I actually had that evening off from work. I'd never done anything like that but was intrigued by the opportunity, and so, when I got home, I pulled up the website and signed up. I was excited to experience it!

As usual, because of the Virgo in me, I was the first to arrive. The shop owner was there, and so was a woman who was the hypnotherapist. She seemed warm hearted and I could see a purple aura around her head, which suggests a strong connection to universal energy.

We sat and chatted until another lady came in who had done this previously. Then a petite, blonde-haired lady with blue eyes came in. She was running late, was flustered, and she told us what happened that caused her to be late. The therapist soothed her with funny anecdotes, and I stood up and gave her a hug.

Soon after that, another woman arrived, and we were ready to begin. The therapist began to tell us about hypnosis and what we could expect, although she made it clear that different people have different experiences. When it comes to connecting to Source, that's always true—we all have different experiences.

We started with meditation, followed by soothing hypnotic suggestions. I dropped down into trance, and soon my body felt very heavy. Ironically, I also felt as though my head was floating.

Then the hypnotist directed us to go back to a childhood memory.

Mine was so random, I don't think I'd ever thought about it before. As a child in California, my dad used to take us to a high school with an open field where we would fly kites. The image that came to me was my dad—young, with a mustache. I must have been about six or seven years old, and we were flying a kite. I remember looking up at him, and he looked down at me and smiled. I felt so peaceful and knew this memory was a gift from the Universe.

Then the hypnotist took us back into the womb. I don't really remember anything—just that it was peaceful.

Next, she guided us back to a past life. I began seeing images in first person, as though I was looking through my own eyes. I was lying on the ground looking up at the blue sky, which was bordered with a few trees I didn't recognize. I sat up and scooted myself toward a small rock ledge and placed my feet on the ground below. I saw ancient sandals on a man's feet, and the feet and the sandals were dusty. I looked down at my hands and turned them in different directions to get a good look at them. They were strong hands, dusty, and very dry.

I then looked to the left and noticed I was in a desert area. I then looked to the right, and saw a woman sitting next to me. She had on a head covering and her eyes were light blue and piercing. She was my wife.

The therapist then took us to another location, a public place. My wife and I were at some sort of sporting event. I looked around and saw that nothing much was happening. Then she had us go to another location, and I was inside a pyramid. I had tools in my hand and was etching out writings.

I was a writer back then, too, it seems.

Then she had us go to our death—assuming we wanted to see it, which I did. I was no longer inside the head of the person in that life, looking out through his eyes. I was in the third person mode up in the corner of the room looking down.

I was lying on an ancient bed, and my wife was sitting next to me. I didn't look old. Following my last breath, I saw a white light orb come up out of my body. Then a large white light orb appeared and they were gone.

I must have died from some type of illness. In my visualizations, I never spoke or heard a voice, although some people do.

After the hypnosis session had concluded, the hypnotist had us write down everything we saw and could remember. I was able to do so easily because it was all perfectly clear. Then she went around the room and asked us to say what we'd seen.

The blonde woman who had come in at the beginning in a fluster, was first. She began to tell what she remembered from her childhood, then in the womb. Then she got to her past life story and things got crazy. She said she was in an ancient desert area. When she looked down at her feet, she had on sandals and her feet were dusty. Then she said she went from seeing in the first person to the third person, looking at her face. She said, "I had the bluest eyes... "

I was losing it—thinking there was no way.

I was next, and I said, "I wrote all of this down so there's proof, and you'll understand why I say there's proof after I tell it."

After I'd shared my visions, the therapist said, "Well, it seems as if you shared a life together."

Following the session, my new friend and I talked. She was born and raised in the same area of California that I was. She moved to Tennessee in the late 1980s, which was synchronistic. The feeling came over me that she was in my soul tribe—the very thing I'd asked my angels for that prior morning.

We exchanged phone numbers and began to text like we were high school girls. Where I have my spiritual gifts, she has hers. Hers is astrology, and so, of course, we told each other our birth signs. She's a Taurus. I'm a Virgo, both earth signs. She asked me for my birthdate, time of birth and location, and then sent me a complete birth chart.

We aren't done, however, with the coincidences. She told me I have three planets in my twelfth house, which makes me a twelfth house angel. She, on the other hand, has three planets in her eighth house, which make her an eighth house phoenix. This was something else that connected us. We'd had a life together, are a part of the same soul tribe, and are deeply connected on a spiritual level. We've now found each other and will begin to live out the contracts we have together in this life. There's a path we're supposed to journey together, and I was told that would happen in the year of eight, which of course is 2024, which adds up to eight.

I'm excited for all of this to come together.

Returning to the topic of this chapter, meditation, once you begin the practice, the shift within is going to happen. Your mind will shift from worry and overthinking, to actually living—free from your obsessive, ego mind. Be strong in your determination to become good at meditation. It's not easy to go through all of the stages of spiritual awakening, especially to get to the point of keeping your frequency at the heightened level of constant connection, but meditation is the tool to use in order to succeed.

The spiritual journey is one of healing first, and that healing is often hard to endure, and at times, it's hard to accept. Rest assured, however, once you get through it and your transformation is complete, the lessons you go through may not become easier, but you will be better equipped to handle them. Going through awakening, doing your meditation in order to connect, and being open to what you're called to do is what's important. It might be a path you're to walk, or it simply might be to be obedient to certain tasks. Whatever your calling, meditation will break down the walls around you and allow you to walk in love. It will allow your Light to be a beacon of hope and for you to pour out love on those who may be searching.

The healing path is difficult, and so you may feel hesitant to go down it. But it is, and it will be worth it. We will need many Lightworkers in the years to come. People are beginning to question what they have known their entire lives, and I certain it's because Source is calling on individuals to search for themselves and no longer to accept the status quo. We're being called to walk away from the aspects of ourselves that no longer align with what we feel vibrationally. We're being called to step onto a new level of intimacy with Source and with each other. We are all called to be love itself—to love who we are, to love the world around us, and to love those who are going through life with us—family and strangers alike. The journey we are on is not intended to be taken alone. Everyone who can walk over the bridge with you needs to be embraced.

Chapter Ten
Be the Bridge

A beautiful aspect of life is that you are encouraged by Source to be who you desire to be and to become who you feel you need to become. It's important to realize that your desire is in line with your calling from Source. The ability to manifest the life you want can and will happen once you connect fully to your own Life Force. Most live their lives holding back because they fear being judged. Whether you're the fearful one, or the one that judges, your impulse is misplaced. When you judge someone else, you don't define them, you define yourself. When you hold back because of fear, you're squandering a precious opportunity Source has provided.

Since I decided to boldly share my true essence and my story, I have been amazed at the number of people I've spoken to who are already on, or have just started on their spiritual journey. So many people are awakening and seeing signs that the Universe wants to communicate with them. Something many share is that they are afraid to say anything to anyone that they're related to, or close with, because they fear being judged—they're afraid of becoming an outcast shunned by friends and family. Similar fears held me back as well. They held me back until I decided that my service to Source and my service to other souls was more important than the relationships I might lose. So I shed the fear of being judged. If someone doesn't want you in their life because you've changed how you think, and now you think differently than they do, I'd say "Goodbye" with love for them. Do this, and you'll open the door wide to finding your true self, and you'll make room for who and what is meant to be in your life.

It's important to embrace your differences completely because you have become and are becoming a better person. Moreover, by embracing your transformation, the essence of who you truly are will create a harmonious life for you. It will also help to create a bridge of energy from your heart that will reach out to others. This can create positive change not only in the lives of those around you, it can also create a positive energetic shift in your community, our nation, and ultimately the world.

We need to leave behind the idea that everyone has to be the same. We all need to be authentic to who we are! Imagine how boring it would be if every flower, every bird, every dog or cat, or every area of the world was the same. We each have different points of view and different perspectives on just about everything, which doesn't mean we are all right or all wrong. It certainly doesn't mean we have to fight about it. Many people believe everything should conform to a certain standard, but the question to ask those who think so is, "Who gets to decide?"

We, as individuals, have no real control over what others do, feel or say, but we do have the ability to control our own lives. We also have a voice that, if used in a loving way, can change the circumstances of our lives and those around us. When we refuse to be open to what someone else tells us about their views and opinions on religion, politics or lifestyle, we cut ourselves off from the level of understanding needed to be a conduit for Source energy. Being open and understanding is required in order to be fully aligned in love.

Source is open to all of us. Really think about that. The Universe is massive. Just try to wrap your mind around the reality that the earth has been revolving around the sun for billions of years. Now think about the countless souls that have come to live on this earth and how many times each soul has incarnated. Consider that every thought and action in each life of each soul is documented in the Akashic Records.

Do you realize that in each lifetime you have been a different person, often with a different gender, ethnicity, ideals and culture, and in many cases the follower of a different religion? Yet so many people continue to live in a small-minded way, thinking they have all of the answers, when in reality, none of us do.

The Archangels are telling me to let you know that what is given to me as my truth may not resonate with you. Each of us is given exactly what we need. Your way is the right way for you, but it may not be the right way for your neighbor. At different points in history, uniformity was the norm and was how most people lived. This created unhappiness for many. People got married because they believed that was what they were supposed to do. Later some realized they'd settled for less than they should have, or that they were gay and now had to live a lie. Some were born into religions they didn't align with and were raised to believe that if they went against the dogma they'd burn in hell. That certainly made for an unhappy life.

Society impressed upon people the need to finish school, get married, buy a house, have children, work the same job, stay married even if they were unhappy, retire and if they were lucky, sit on the front porch and watch the world go by until they finally kicked the bucket. Not long ago that's literally how most people lived, but thankfully that mindset is shifting. People are becoming aware that there is more to life than simply blending in. There's a growing realization that we have a choice to be who we are and to do it in our own way. Thankfully, we are learning to be accepting of others, regardless of our differences. We're blazing new trails. It's been a long road to get where we are today, and there's certainly more work to be done. Being used by Source to create a change in a quest to spread love is true abundance—an abundance that we share energetically. Finding the peace of where you are currently, is true abundance. Once you make peace with the present moment, joy and gratitude will follow, and the ability to vibrate at the love frequency will increase exponentially.

We are all One collective, especially as we become more love centered—One with all, One as all, One is all. The place to find true unity is in our hearts. Those embers glowing in your heart space are gently asking you to look to Source so that Source will lightly blow the breath of love on them and create a blazing fire.

It is impossible to teach the meaning of love—it cannot be taught. It may feel like an emotion, but in reality, it is the vibration we achieve when we are in alignment with Source energy and experience joy as a result. To reach this level of alignment, your human self must hold the hand of your divine being to navigate through your 3-D life, to gain the knowledge that will create the ability to stand in both realms. Call out to the angels, guides and ancestors who surround and guide you.

You were born with a calling to pursue in this life. Your soul decided on it before you were born. The spirit realm and the guides and angels that surround you will help you find the right path and then push you forward on it. But you must be attentive and be willing to be led by the urges they plant in you. The spiritual teacher, Joseph Campbell, who was born in 1904 and died in 1987, was often asked by his students at Sarah Lawrence University what they should do with their lives. His answer was always the same: "Follow your bliss!"

Why don't we pursue our bliss? We have free will, which means we can do so, but we can also be stubborn—with the result that we may totally ignore the urges and our intuition. Perhaps society, friends and family have influenced us to go in a different way. Those are reasons it can take years, perhaps even decades of missteps before you feel the wind at your back. Rest assured, nonetheless, it's never too late to get on the right path. Everything that has happened in your life was intended. There is a way from where you are to where you need to be. Acceptance of where you are is the place to start. Then plot your course to a life of joy, peace and love.

In my experience, the "mistakes" I thought I made, were actually the most defining times in my life. Looking back, I realize there's purpose in struggle. Struggle results in growth—it forces us to change. Such times taught me who I am and to have compassion and understanding without judgment for others in similar situations.

In short, things will become easier if you accept the difficult times—those that occurred in the past and those yet to come. Realize what you learned from past difficulties and how much you have evolved and matured as a result. Embrace them and forgive yourself and others who may have played a role in creating what was a difficult time. As discussed in previous chapters, it's the forgiveness of yourself and others that heals past traumas. Then practice being present in the only moment that actually exists—the NOW—and allow yourself to be led onto a path of abundance and a life well lived.

Concerning the future, it's important to change how you look at things. Change the way you respond to situations and to people. Change the way you feel about yourself and your life. Lighten up. Smile a lot. Laugh at the ironies of life. When your mind is set to look at situations or happenings as being intended, instead of tirelessly worrying or stressing, your life will start to shift and become more positive.

Like attracts like, remember? Life is a mirror of your thoughts and beliefs so discard the idea that things are working against you. Change your outlook to "whatever happens is in my best interest." Realize that Divine Love will meet every single one of your human needs and then some, if you allow it and expect it.

Since I have changed the way I think about circumstances, situations and people, doors open for me all of the time. I believe this is because people see you differently and are more open to you when you carry the Light within. Those who still live in the shadows may dislike you for no reason, and that's a compliment to your Light—remember that. When you are a beacon of Light working for Source and loving humanity, you are seen as different. As you do this, you touch the souls of others, which plants the seeds of love. You really never know if you are the one preparing the soil, planting the seeds, watering, spreading sunshine or bringing in the harvest. But as a collective consciousness, we are working together to bring all of humanity into the Light. Never think of your part in the shift of the world as being too small. Even small gestures of love, compassion and gratitude will bring about positive changes in individual souls.

You never know how one word you're prompted to say might change the trajectory of someone's path, or even your own. I "innerstand" now in my own life that when I follow those intuitive promptings the Divine will entrust me with more. I receive more intentional guidance on my path. I hear and see more from the spirit realm to help assist another. The Archangels speak to my heart and bless me with a knowing of the direction I need to go for my best interests and to help humanity.

I'll say it all day long, the Archangels desire us to call on them for anything. They have become my best friends. I never feel alone, even in times of solitude, because their presence is so full. Don't forget, an "Arch" is the bridge to connect the head to the heart. That is exactly what the Archangels are, a bridge to the heart.

When you look at the world and see people as a work of God, you begin to feel a bond and a connection. We all go through similar trials. We all understand what it feels like to experience every human emotion—joy, sorrow, grief, and pity. We all know what it feels like to be in the presence of pure love—or in another's disdain. We all strive at times to be the best version of ourselves, and yet, we have all viewed ourselves as not good enough, or incapable of performing a certain task. We use labels to create division between us. We are all labeled with a gender at birth. We're given a name and a number that defines us. We are handed a religion and beliefs, and we are taught what to think of different skin tones, cultures, politics, lifestyles and education.

As we grow into who we are, we must have the courage to push back and question everything. We must realize we have our own path and sometimes that will mean going against the status quo and ruffling a few feathers along the way. Because when we are called to this earth, it is with a purpose to be true to who we are and to be co-creators with every loving collective energy to bring about the new earth.

When we consider the different spiritual teachers down through the ages, they all have exhibited a level of peace that surely comes from the Divine. They all have exhibited a level of wisdom that was easy for our souls to understand, and yet was deeply insightful with respect to human nature. Each taught that forming a connection to a higher power or higher self is the key to finding joy and harmony in one's life.

After spending the years deep diving into the different religious teachings, I realize we don't have to be the same, or to believe the same to know the presence of peace that can only come from Source. No matter what their faith was, each of those teachers demonstrated what we are capable of if we will just sit introspectively and wait, knowing we will get an answer. Many problems come about that could be avoided if we'd simply waited for guidance. We tend to rely on our own understanding and then our human nature takes control. This leads to confusion most of the time, because we are trying to force something to happen that isn't meant for us. I'm guilty of having done this before my awakening. Now I'm more patient and know that if it is meant for me, it will not pass me by.

Jesus said, "It is the pure in heart who will see God." Insight into Source comes from a pure heart, and from love and humility. The more we live our own truth, the more insight we are given. Many times the answers come to us from others, but nowadays few people bother to listen. I recently have been experiencing more garrulous people when attempting conversation. There are those who tend to believe everyone wants to hear what they have to say. We need to open ourselves up to having reciprocal conversations that fill everyone's cup.

The Buddha says, "Speak in such a way that others love to listen to you. Listen in such a way that others love to speak to you." It's a simple concept. Just be as open and eager to hear what someone else is saying as you are to share your own thoughts.

The Buddha also says, "The quieter you become, the more you can hear." The more you meditate the more you will hear from your angels, Source, and your higher self. When we are on the edge of our seat, expecting to hear those divine messages, we can't. It's because we have a chatty mind that won't allow the thoughts to flow through to us. Being at peace with yourself is an important part of being at peace with less speaking and more listening.

Allow me to share an experience I had yesterday that exhibits the value of being open to listening to guidance of the spiritual realm. For about two weeks I'd been hearing from my angels that I needed to be careful about distractions. I needed to be aware of new "devils" that would try to come in when I hit new higher levels. I'd also been told that a new divine love was coming to me, and also the coming year was going to offer a huge opportunity not only for my life, but for the lives of those who are following their calling.

I woke up on a Saturday morning, and as I was talking to my angels and to Source, I said, "My book will be done on Christmas Day, so I need guidance on what path I take next. I need a mentor and how to get this published."

I heard, "Listen closely to words, the path will come to you and be shown to you." I woke up Sunday and went to work. It was Christmas Eve and activity at the restaurant was much slower than normal. I was doing server checkouts at the bar area, and there was a gentleman sitting there talking to the bartender. He started talking about the time he lived in Germany. I chimed in and asked where he lived because I have family there. So we chatted for about 15 minutes, then I had to get some other things done before we closed. I walked back behind the bar and he handed me a napkin with his phone number on it. Then he left. I really wasn't sure if I ought to call or not, but he was attractive, looked successful, and was just a bit older than I am.

After he left, a couple came in. I walked back behind the bar to do another server checkout and the woman said, "I love your ugly Christmas sweater! May I take a picture of it?"

I posed, and we laughed and struck up a conversation. She was full of life and joy.

She looked at me and said, "You are full of so much light and I love your smile."

I told her I felt the same about her. Her vibration was absolutely infectious and fun.

When she was 14 she had lost a leg to cancer. She had a bionic leg that didn't slow her down. She said, "I am a motivational and keynote speaker, and have written several books—"

When she said that, I felt that feeling I get when it is a divine meeting. I felt as if warm water was being poured out over my head and running down my body.

I said, "You do what?"

And she said it again. I explained that we had a divine appointment at that moment. Luckily, she knew what I meant, and we talked. I told her I was told by Source and my angels that I will be doing keynote speaking and publishing a book.

She didn't even blink when I said that and was open to the concept of someone being spoken to divinely. Well, I made a new friend who will help mentor me through this process. I knew it was coming, I didn't know when, where, who or how, I just knew to be open to listening for answers and direction.

I heard the warning from the angels to listen because I quieted my mind, and I heard the message from my new friend because I was listening to hear what she was saying.

By the way, I did send the guy that gave me his number a text when I left work. He called me that evening and we chatted. He was funny, successful and financially well off, attractive, and he loves to travel. But he also likes to drink, is into politics and is not a great listener. He was all over dating sites and was desperate to find a partner. In other words, I saw some very red flags I swore I'd never ignore again. I'm serious about the type of person I desire in my life, and I know Source has whomever it is set aside for me. So, I told him that I knew he wasn't intended for me and wished him well.

I was proud of myself. The Kim of five years ago would not have thought about whether he was good for me or not, but now I know I need someone of equal frequency and nothing less, and that is what will come into my life. I also believe he was sent as one of the distractions I was warned about—if I focus on the wrong person, the right one might be missed—another reason why being in tune with your intuition is so important for your soul's evolution. Intuition will not steer you wrong.

With all of that being said, open yourself up to listening to your inner guidance, to Source and to other people and thereby save yourself both time and heartache. On the positive side, you will possibly be making new connections that may assist you on the path of your calling.

So many opportunities pop up in front of us that we may overlook if we are too busy to notice, or perhaps the person is not what we're expecting and we turn away. To truly embrace your calling, you need to embrace and be open to others. This is where building the bridge from my heart to yours and yours to another begins. Putting labels on people who are different from us needs to cease along with the other old fashioned thoughts we have. When we put Source at our center, we see through the lens of pure love. Booker T.

Washington said, "I shall allow no man to belittle my soul by making me hate him." When we aren't in alignment with Source energy, we allow in those who are against us and we end up with ill will and hatred towards them.

On the spiritual path, you figure out how to alchemize those emotions. In turn, you become more understanding and realize there's something unhealed in most people, and that they may be struggling within themselves. People who live in darkness are full of unhealed trauma, generational curses and ancestral wounding. They typically are holding onto whatever they can and want to at least feel something. Many would be totally numb if they didn't feel hate or bitterness inside. Showing them compassion and understanding will allow the love of Source to be shown through you.

I am not saying you should allow yourself to be abused. Healthy boundaries are one of the most important aspects of living a spiritual life. What I am saying is, if you don't partake in the drama of these people and understand they're coming from a place where you have been at one time, it becomes easier to ask Source to heal them. If your vibration is high, and you are on the love frequency, your energy can begin to flow healing energies towards them. In this way, you can help them, and they won't even be aware of it.

The vibration we put out into the world can either lift it up or bring it down. Have you ever been somewhere and when Debbie Downer shows up or the guy you work with walks in and the energy of the room changes entirely? This also happens when you show up and light up the room. That Light becomes infectious and over time it changes people. Their true nature begins to surface, and their Light begins to shine.

When we show up and share Light energy with others, it raises the vibration not only of our environment, it changes the vibration of the outer world, too. When we accept others for who they are, and just love them anyway, it not only raises the vibration within us, but also in them. People come up against so many challenges in life that there's a huge need to show love and acceptance. If we allow Source to speak into us and live with those words within us, we then can share those words with others to lift them up as well. When I speak and teach about being a bridge of love, I am a voice for Source and the angelic realm. In truth, we all are.

To be a bridge of love begins with understanding and compassion. Your heart needs to be open and full of grace. When we reach out and help each other, we are being examples of "God Love." As we look to religious teachings, they are centered around the base of the tree. Each branch that extends out of it is a strong branch that Source created to show us that we are all the same. All have the same roots and the same base.

There is much dissension in the world because people believe in the egoic thought that their religion is the absolute right religion. I am here to tell you, there is no right nor wrong. All of these religions were created and written by humans, but the center of each one is the same in all. They look to a Higher Power or Higher Self.

Think about this. If you put people of differing political views in a room and didn't let them know about their differences, they would all be polite and kind—until the political talk surfaced. Then they'd become enemies. The thing is, they may vote differently, but the core of their beliefs is generally a love for their country. That love for country is LOVE, and that is the base of the politics of each individual. Everything else that is put out there is sent by the darkness. The incessant arguments blind us from seeing the basic truth of the core belief.

We also need to build a bridge of equality between races and cultures. We need to build a bridge of acceptance for our LGBTQ community. We need to build a bridge for those with mental illness. We need to build a bridge for the homeless. These bridges are free. They are free because love is free. If you set your opinions down and look past the differences you see in another, bridges of love can and will be built by the hand of Source. It all begins within us, it will all begin with love as small as a mustard seed. It is imperative to drop your ego, and to drop the labels that cause the divide. We are truly One. We are truly the same, and we are all here for the same purpose—to find our purpose and love each other. Think how many people in history may have missed their calling because of pride and bigotry. Think how many times you might have been a blessing to someone but you were not because you were emotionally closed off because of differences.

Being a bridge of love is freedom for your soul, and it is freedom for all of humanity. You may ask how one person can change the world. I say, "How many individuals have changed the world?" If you look back at the teachers of faith, they changed the world.

There are inventors from days gone by who have changed the world. There are inventors today who are changing the world. There are thoughts, voices and prayers that change the world. If you are a force for good, and you are willing to go down the spiritual path of healing, you will definitely change the world with your thoughts and higher vibration. We are asked nothing more from our Creator than to be a beacon of love for others to come to in times of need. We are asked to be as Jesus was and is, which is to accept everyone with open arms and compassion. We are to be as peaceful and mindful as the Buddha and to share our wisdom with those who may need it as he did. We are called to stand in our power and believe in ourselves as Krishna taught Arjuna on the battlefield. We are to be givers of love, of Light, of compassion, of patience, of gratitude, of hope, of joy, of peace and of kindness.

There is nothing that comes from this world that compares with what you receive from God. All that we need is there for us. We are only asked to be in alignment with all that is good and with our God frequency. We are asked to be who we are and be so with love in our hearts.

Be a bridge that others can cross over with loving guidance to see that the world is a loving and caring place. We are in a beautiful time of transition. We are bringing about a new world—a world of love, peace and joy.

Be the Bridge, Because We Are All One in Love.

Conclusion

All of the moments in your life are perfect. Even those brutal ones you felt as though you might not get through. They are perfect because they were all meant to happen in order to propel you forward on your journey. Those moments that were the most scary, painful, or seemingly catastrophic were what created a depth of character, maturity, and wisdom in you. They were lessons you needed on your path to bring you where you are today. It was hard to go through them, but if you will shift how you think about them, you may actually remember them fondly when you are farther along the road of life.

Perfect moments have led you to the next stage of your journey. The German philosopher, Arthur Schopenhauer, who was born in 1788 and died in 1860, said that when it's happening, life seems chaotic. But when you look back, especially from old age, it appears to have unfolded according to a predetermined plan.

Take a moment now and look back. Can't you see the perfection of the plan—how things happened in ways that now seem to have been predictable? How things happened just as they had to in order to get you to where you are now, which is just where you need to be in order to take part in the Great Awakening?

Take a moment now to determine where you are vibrationally. Your level of vibration will determine whether your life will be negative or positive. If the level is not where it needs to be, shift your thoughts and beliefs into a positive mode. Jettison any idea or inkling that you are a victim.

Know that good things are flowing to you—truly know it and they will. Stepping into a positive sense of flow will create positive outcomes for you now and in the future.

When Source told me I was going to write this book, I pushed back saying I wasn't capable of it. I had tried in the past, but never got anywhere. Nevertheless, I was assured I would be put on the proper course to achieve this goal. And true to everything Source indicates, it came to fruition—not according to my timing, but according to divine timing. In the three months it took me to write this book, each chapter was revealed to me just when it needed to be. As I was writing, something would happen that I could use at the very moment I needed it. Journal entries I'd written during the past few years became the raw material for chapters. Words flowed from me, I strung them together, and before I knew it, the book was done. I thought before, but now I know that with God all things are possible. I know this with deep faith and trust, and I am grateful for the growth I have experienced during the time it took to write this book.

As I look through the chapters, I am shown the truth in each. The truth, my truth that Source saw fit to show me.

We all come from the same tree, and together we can assure that the roots, trunk and branches are strong. We all know intrinsically that we should treat others with respect. As we break down walls that separate us, we must forgive and heal, not only our wounds, but the wounds of the collective. We must make friends with our ego selves and calm their fears in order to create a positive world. When we release fear, we live in love, and to live in love is powerful—power is generated that creates an ever higher vibration and frequency that will keep us all connected to Source.

Walking in truth will open the way to create the life you desire. That truth will also show you just how chosen you are. You were born to be here during this exact time, in this incarnation, to be a player in this age of world transformation. Living in gratitude and completely surrendering not only will change your life, it will change the lives of those on the opposite side of the planet. Once you give yourself over to Source, you will begin to feel the fire within, and the flame within you will grow.

Kindle a deep sense of love for yourself. Through meditation seek guidance from Source and your spirit team, and join with me to create a bridge of love for each of us all over the world to cross over.

If one person can create an energetic positive change, just imagine the amount of change we can create together for the collective of humanity. Radiate the frequency of love everywhere you go and help generate the energy that will bring about a new world of love, peace and joy. It really is possible, so have faith that it is, and expect positive change to come. Be the Bridge United in One Love.

If you enjoyed this book here are a few more from The Oaklea Press you'll want to read:

The author interviewed more than 100 experts in fields from quantum physics to consciousness research to develop an airtight case for the continuation of human consciousness after bodily death—a case he believes an open-minded individual will find impossible to refute. If you have any doubts about life after death, this is absolutely a must read.

Kindle: ASIN: B0CBS3PNZ8
PB: ISISBN-13: 978-1892538727

All the knowledge of the universe resides within you because at a deep level all minds, past and present, are connected. Everything that has ever happened, every thought, every idea is there. The trick is to draw out information when you need it. In this book Stephen explains how he learned to do so and how you can, too.

Kindle: ASIN: B07HHFFWP8
Paperback: ISBN-10: 1723835250

This 5-Star rated, fast-paced thriller is based on the true nature of reality as revealed in the book you hold in your hands. The heroine travels to the Caribbean Island of Martinque to save her father and learns the secret of life in the process. A page-turner, this novel won First Place for Fiction from *Writer's Digest* and First Place for Visionary Fiction from *Independent Publisher* magazine.

Kindle: ASIN: B08S7MG4WM
Paperback: ASIN: B08SB6VG9L

Made in the USA
Columbia, SC
04 July 2024

d4662fe4-250d-4d43-b6cd-9bc3b1743b32R01